Mastering
DATA SCIENCE
AND BIG DATA ANALYTICS
Concepts, Techniques, and Applications

Nikhilesh Mishra
Author

Website
www.nikhileshmishra.com

Copyright Information

Dedication

This book is lovingly dedicated to the cherished memory of my father, **Late Krishna Gopal Mishra**, and my mother**, Mrs. Vijay Kanti Mishra.** Their unwavering support, guidance, and love continue to inspire me.

Table of Contents

Author's Preface

Welcome to the captivating world of the knowledge we are about to explore! Within these pages, we invite you to embark on a journey that delves into the frontiers of information and understanding.

Charting the Path to Knowledge

Dive deep into the subjects we are about to explore as we unravel the intricate threads of innovation, creativity, and problem-solving. Whether you're a curious enthusiast, a seasoned professional, or an eager learner, this book serves as your gateway to gaining a deeper understanding.

Your Guiding Light

From the foundational principles of our chosen field to the advanced frontiers of its applications, we've meticulously crafted this book to be your trusted companion. Each chapter is an expedition, guided by expertise and filled with practical insights to empower you on your quest for knowledge.

What Awaits You

- **Illuminate the Origins:** Embark on a journey through the historical evolution of our chosen field, discovering key milestones that have paved the way for breakthroughs.

- **Demystify Complex Concepts:** Grasp the fundamental principles, navigate intricate concepts, and explore practical applications.

- **Mastery of the Craft:** Equip yourself with the skills and knowledge needed to excel in our chosen domain.

Your Journey Begins Here

As we embark on this enlightening journey together, remember that mastery is not just about knowledge but also the wisdom to apply it. Let each chapter be a stepping stone towards unlocking your potential, and let this book be your guide to becoming a true connoisseur of our chosen field.

So, turn the page, delve into the chapters, and immerse yourself in the world of knowledge. Let curiosity be your compass, and let the pursuit of understanding be your guide.

Begin your expedition now. Your quest for mastery awaits!

Sincerely,

Nikhilesh Mishra,

Author

PART I

Introduction to Data Science and Big data Analytics

CHAPTER 1

Introduction to Data Science

In today's data-driven world, the field of Data Science stands as a powerful beacon, illuminating the path to unlocking invaluable insights from the vast and complex seas of data that surround us. Data Science is not merely a discipline; it's a revolution that empowers professionals, researchers, enthusiasts, and fresh minds alike to harness the true potential of data.

At its core, Data Science is the art and science of transforming raw data into meaningful and actionable knowledge. It weaves together a symphony of techniques from various domains, including statistics, computer science, and domain expertise, to extract hidden patterns, predict future trends, and make informed decisions.

In this journey of discovery, Data Scientists play a pivotal role as modern-day explorers. They delve deep into the data wilderness, armed with cutting-edge tools and methodologies, to unveil the stories hidden within. Whether it's uncovering customer preferences, predicting stock market trends, diagnosing diseases, or optimizing supply chains, Data Science's reach is as limitless as the imagination itself.

In the pages that follow, we will embark on a comprehensive exploration of the realm of Data Science. We will decipher the key concepts, demystify the terminologies, and unveil the roles and responsibilities that define this dynamic field. Through a holistic journey, we will unravel the intricacies of data acquisition, preprocessing, exploration, and analysis, equipping you with the skills and insights necessary to navigate the ever-evolving landscape of Data Science.

Welcome to a world where data isn't just a collection of ones and zeros; it's a narrative waiting to be told, a puzzle eager to be solved, and a gateway to informed decision-making. As we embark on this enlightening voyage, we invite you to immerse yourself in the captivating realm of Data Science and embark on a journey of mastery that promises to empower, inspire, and transform.

A. Defining Data Science and Its Significance

In an era where data flows like an inexhaustible river, Data Science emerges as the compass that guides us through its depths. Data Science can be understood as the interdisciplinary field that amalgamates statistical analysis, machine learning, domain expertise, and technological prowess to extract actionable insights and knowledge from data, both big and small. It encompasses a broad spectrum of activities, from data collection and preprocessing to advanced analytics and visualization, culminating in the transformation of raw information into valuable intelligence.

At its heart, Data Science is not just about crunching numbers; it's about unraveling the narratives concealed within data streams, unveiling patterns, trends, and correlations that empower organizations and individuals to make informed decisions. This field is driven by a blend of technical proficiency, creative problem-solving, and the ability to ask the right questions that lead to groundbreaking discoveries.

Key Aspects of Data Science:

1.   **Data Collection and Preparation:** Data Science commences with the acquisition of diverse and often voluminous datasets from various sources, such as sensors, social media, transaction records, and more. These datasets, often characterized by their volume, variety, and velocity, must be carefully curated, cleaned, and transformed into a format suitable for analysis. Data Scientists play a crucial role in ensuring the quality and integrity of the data they work with.

2.   **Exploratory Data Analysis (EDA):** EDA is the process of visually and statistically exploring data to uncover meaningful patterns, relationships, and anomalies. It involves generating summary statistics, creating visualizations, and conducting initial hypothesis testing to guide further analysis. EDA helps Data Scientists gain an understanding of the data's

characteristics and potential insights.

3. **Machine Learning and Predictive Modeling:** Machine learning algorithms lie at the heart of many Data Science applications. These algorithms learn from historical data to make predictions or decisions without being explicitly programmed. They can be used for tasks such as image recognition, natural language processing, recommendation systems, fraud detection, and much more.

4. **Data Visualization and Communication:** The ability to effectively communicate insights derived from data is paramount. Data Scientists utilize data visualization techniques to present complex information in an easily understandable and visually appealing manner. Visualizations help stakeholders grasp patterns and trends, facilitating data-driven decision-making.

5. **Ethics and Privacy:** As data becomes more accessible, ethical considerations surrounding its collection, storage, and use have gained prominence. Data Scientists are responsible for handling data ethically, ensuring privacy, and safeguarding sensitive information.

The Significance of Data Science:

The significance of Data Science extends across industries, academia, and society at large:

1. **Business Transformation:** Organizations leverage Data Science to optimize operations, enhance customer experiences, and make strategic decisions. It enables businesses to predict market trends, tailor marketing campaigns, optimize supply chains, and identify new revenue opportunities.

2. **Healthcare Advancements:** Data Science is revolutionizing healthcare by enabling personalized medicine, disease prediction, drug discovery, and patient outcome analysis. It empowers medical professionals to make data-driven diagnoses and treatment plans.

3. **Scientific Discoveries**: Researchers across domains use Data Science to analyze massive datasets, uncover patterns, and formulate hypotheses. It accelerates scientific discoveries by facilitating data-intensive research.

4. **Social Impact:** Data Science contributes to addressing societal challenges, such as climate change, poverty, and disaster response. It aids in predicting natural disasters, optimizing resource allocation, and designing targeted interventions.

5. **Career Opportunities:** The demand for Data Scientists has surged, with a shortage of skilled professionals in the field. Data Science offers diverse career paths, from analysts and engineers to researchers and consultants.

In essence, Data Science is the compass that guides us through the data landscape, unlocking insights and driving innovation. Its interdisciplinary nature and far-reaching applications position it as a cornerstone of the modern age, empowering individuals and organizations to navigate the complexities of an increasingly data-centric world. As we delve deeper into the world of Data Science, we will unravel its intricacies and equip you with the knowledge and tools needed to harness its transformative potential.

B. Roles and Responsibilities of Data Scientists

In the digital age, where data reigns supreme, Data Scientists emerge as the architects of insight, wielding their analytical prowess to extract value from the vast sea of information. A Data Scientist's role is multifaceted, demanding a blend of technical acumen, domain expertise, and creative problem-solving. Let's delve into the in-depth roles and responsibilities that define this dynamic profession.

1. **Data Collection and Exploration:** Data Scientists are responsible for sourcing and acquiring relevant datasets for analysis. This involves understanding the data needs of the project, identifying potential sources, and designing data collection methods. They must possess the skills to clean, preprocess, and transform raw data into usable formats, ensuring data quality and integrity.

2. **Hypothesis Generation and Testing:** Data Scientists

formulate hypotheses and design experiments to test them. They apply statistical techniques and hypothesis testing to draw meaningful insights from data. This process requires a deep understanding of the problem domain and the ability to translate real-world questions into actionable data analysis tasks.

3. **Exploratory Data Analysis (EDA):** EDA forms a pivotal phase in the Data Scientist's journey. They use visualization tools and statistical techniques to uncover patterns, trends, and anomalies within the data. EDA sets the stage for subsequent analysis and provides crucial insights that drive decision-making.

4. **Machine Learning and Modeling:** Data Scientists develop and implement machine learning models to solve complex problems. They select appropriate algorithms, fine-tune model parameters, and optimize model performance. Whether it's building predictive models, classification systems, recommendation engines, or natural language processing applications, Data Scientists are at the forefront of applying cutting-edge techniques.

5. **Feature Engineering and Selection:** Feature engineering involves identifying and creating relevant variables that enhance model performance. Data Scientists must possess domain knowledge to engineer features that capture the essence of the problem. They also employ techniques to select the most informative features, ensuring optimal model performance.

6. **Model Evaluation and Interpretation:** Data Scientists assess the performance of their models using various metrics and validation techniques. They interpret model results, identifying strengths, weaknesses, and potential areas of improvement. Model interpretation is crucial for ensuring transparency and reliability in decision-making.

7. **Deployment and Integration:** Bringing a model from the testing environment to real-world applications requires Data Scientists to collaborate with engineers and IT teams. They ensure smooth deployment, integration, and scalability of models within existing systems. This stage demands a blend of technical expertise and effective communication.

8. **Continuous Learning and Innovation:** The field of Data Science evolves rapidly. Data Scientists are lifelong learners, staying updated with the latest techniques, tools, and advancements. They experiment with novel approaches, embrace emerging technologies, and apply innovative strategies to solve challenging problems.

9. **Communication and Stakeholder Engagement**: Data Scientists are adept at conveying complex insights to both technical and non-technical stakeholders. They must communicate findings effectively through reports, presentations, and visualizations. The ability to bridge the gap between data and decision-makers is essential for driving organizational change.

10. **Ethical Considerations:** Data Scientists must navigate ethical dilemmas surrounding data privacy, bias, and fairness. They are responsible for ensuring that their analyses and models uphold ethical standards and do not perpetuate discrimination or harm.

In essence, Data Scientists are the storytellers of data, weaving narratives that inform, guide, and transform. Their roles and responsibilities span the entire data lifecycle, from data collection and exploration to modeling and deployment. As the torchbearers of insight, Data Scientists navigate the complexities of the digital landscape, illuminating the path to data-driven decision-making and innovation.

C. Key Data Science Concepts and Terminology

In the realm of Data Science, a rich tapestry of concepts and terminology interweaves to form the foundation of this dynamic and transformative field. As we embark on this exploration, let's unravel the key concepts that underpin Data Science and the terminology that guides practitioners in their data-driven journey.

1. **Data Types:** Data Scientists work with various data types, including:

- **Numeric Data:** Representing quantitative values, such as age, income, or temperature.

- **Categorical Data:** Representing categories or labels, like gender, color, or city names.

- **Text Data:** Natural language text, used in sentiment analysis, text classification, and more.

- **Time Series Data:** Sequential data points indexed by time, crucial in analyzing trends and forecasting.

2. **Descriptive Statistics:** Descriptive statistics summarize and describe datasets, including measures like mean, median, mode, standard deviation, and percentiles. These metrics provide insights into central tendencies, variability, and distribution of data.

3. **Inferential Statistics:** Inferential statistics involve drawing conclusions about a population based on a sample. Techniques like hypothesis testing and confidence intervals help Data Scientists make educated inferences from limited data.

4. **Probability Distributions:** Probability distributions, such as the normal distribution, binomial distribution, and Poisson distribution, model the likelihood of different outcomes. They play a fundamental role in understanding data variability and making predictions.

5. **Regression Analysis:** Regression analysis models the relationship between a dependent variable and one or more independent variables. Linear regression, for example, estimates

the linear relationship between variables, while more complex forms like polynomial regression capture nonlinear relationships.

6. **Classification Algorithms:** Classification algorithms categorize data into distinct classes or categories. Examples include logistic regression, decision trees, support vector machines, and neural networks. These algorithms find applications in image recognition, spam detection, and medical diagnosis.

7. **Clustering:** Clustering algorithms group similar data points into clusters, revealing underlying patterns. K-means, hierarchical clustering, and DBSCAN are popular techniques used for customer segmentation, anomaly detection, and more.

8. **Feature Selection and Engineering:** Feature selection involves choosing the most relevant variables for a model. Feature engineering creates new features that enhance model performance and capture domain knowledge.

9. **Overfitting and Underfitting:** Overfitting occurs when a model learns noise in the training data, resulting in poor generalization to new data. Underfitting, on the other hand, occurs when a model is too simplistic to capture the underlying patterns in the data.

10. **Bias and Variance:** Bias refers to the error introduced by approximating real-world problems with simplified models.

Variance measures the model's sensitivity to fluctuations in the training data. Achieving a balance between bias and variance is critical for model performance.

11. **Cross-Validation:** Cross-validation assesses a model's performance by dividing the data into training and validation sets multiple times. Techniques like k-fold cross-validation help evaluate model generalization.

12. **Ensemble Methods**: Ensemble methods combine multiple models to improve predictive accuracy and reduce overfitting. Examples include random forests, gradient boosting, and bagging.

13. **Neural Networks and Deep Learning:** Neural networks emulate the human brain's structure and are the foundation of deep learning. Deep learning models, such as convolutional neural networks (CNNs) and recurrent neural networks (RNNs), excel in tasks like image recognition, language processing, and time series analysis.

14. **Bias and Fairness:** Data Scientists address bias and fairness concerns in models, ensuring that predictions do not disproportionately affect certain groups or perpetuate discrimination.

15. **Model Interpretability and Explainability:** As models become more complex, explaining their decisions becomes essential. Techniques like LIME and SHAP enable Data Scientists

to understand and communicate the rationale behind model predictions.

In the intricate tapestry of Data Science, these concepts and terminologies serve as threads that bind together the art and science of extracting knowledge from data. By mastering these foundational elements, Data Scientists wield the tools needed to unravel patterns, predict trends, and shape the future through data-driven insights.

CHAPTER 2

Introduction to Big Data Analytics

In the digital era, data proliferates at an unprecedented pace, reshaping industries, economies, and societies. Amid this deluge of information, Big Data Analytics emerges as the compass that guides us through the vast and intricate landscape of data. At its core, Big Data Analytics is a transformative discipline that harnesses advanced technologies, methodologies, and techniques to extract profound insights from massive, complex, and rapidly evolving datasets.

In this chapter, we embark on a journey into the realm of Big Data Analytics, where we unravel its essence, explore its challenges, and unveil the extraordinary potential it holds. We delve into the fundamental concepts that define Big Data, dissect its inherent characteristics, and navigate the technologies that empower us to tame its unruly nature.

From the boundless streams of social media interactions to the intricate trails of financial transactions, Big Data Analytics illuminates hidden patterns, uncovers latent correlations, and opens doors to informed decision-making. Join us as we traverse the frontiers of this exhilarating domain, unraveling the mysteries of Big Data Analytics and equipping ourselves to navigate the data-rich landscapes that shape our world.

A. Understanding Big Data and Its Challenges

In our interconnected world, data flows ceaselessly from countless sources, ushering us into the era of Big Data. This monumental shift has ignited a revolution in how we perceive, process, and leverage information. Big Data, characterized by its volume, velocity, variety, veracity, and value, represents a treasure trove of potential insights and opportunities. However, alongside its promise lies a set of complex challenges that demand meticulous understanding and strategic solutions.

Defining Big Data: Big Data refers to the vast and diverse collection of structured and unstructured data that exceeds the processing capabilities of traditional database systems. It encompasses three primary dimensions:

1.   **Volume:** Big Data is immense, often exceeding terabytes, petabytes, or even exabytes of data. This scale necessitates innovative storage and processing solutions to manage and analyze such vast quantities.

2.   **Velocity:** Data is generated at unprecedented speeds, often in real-time or near real-time. Streams of data flow from sources like social media, sensors, and IoT devices, requiring efficient processing and analysis mechanisms.

3.   **Variety:** Big Data comes in myriad forms, including text, images, videos, sensor readings, and more. This diversity necessitates adaptable tools and techniques to process and derive meaning from heterogeneous data sources.

Additional V's:

4.   **Veracity:** Veracity refers to the accuracy and reliability of data. Big Data is often noisy, incomplete, or erroneous, posing challenges in ensuring data quality and trustworthiness.

5.   **Value:** The ultimate goal of Big Data is to extract valuable insights that drive decision-making and innovation. The challenge lies in identifying meaningful patterns amidst the noise and transforming data into actionable knowledge.

Challenges of Big Data:

1.   **Storage and Scalability:** Storing and managing massive volumes of data requires scalable and distributed storage solutions. Traditional databases struggle to handle Big Data's scale, leading to the rise of distributed file systems like Hadoop Distributed File System (HDFS) and cloud storage platforms.

2.   **Processing Speed:** Real-time and near real-time data streams demand rapid processing to extract timely insights. Technologies like Apache Spark and in-memory databases enable

high-speed data processing and analysis.

3. **Data Integration:** Combining data from diverse sources can be challenging due to varying formats, structures, and semantics. Data integration tools and techniques are essential to harmonize data for analysis.

4. **Data Variety:** Unstructured and semi-structured data, such as text, images, and videos, pose challenges for analysis. Natural language processing, computer vision, and other techniques are employed to extract insights from these data types.

5. **Data Quality and Veracity:** Data is often noisy, incomplete, or inconsistent. Ensuring data quality through data cleaning, validation, and transformation is critical to deriving accurate insights.

6. **Privacy and Security:** As data volumes grow, ensuring data privacy and security becomes increasingly complex. Protecting sensitive information while enabling data analysis requires robust encryption, access controls, and compliance measures.

7. **Analytical Complexity:** Advanced analytical techniques are needed to extract meaningful patterns from vast and complex datasets. Machine learning algorithms, predictive modeling, and data mining play a pivotal role in uncovering insights.

8.   **Talent and Expertise Gap:** The demand for skilled Big Data professionals often outpaces the supply. Organizations struggle to find experts who possess the interdisciplinary skills required for Big Data analytics.

9.   **Cost Management:** Storing, processing, and analyzing Big Data can incur substantial costs, especially in cloud-based environments. Efficient resource allocation and cost optimization strategies are essential.

10.   **Ethical and Legal Considerations:** The use of Big Data raises ethical concerns around privacy, consent, and potential biases in analysis. Compliance with regulations like GDPR and ethical data handling practices are paramount.

In the dynamic landscape of Big Data, the challenges are as diverse and intricate as the data itself. Navigating these challenges demands a multidisciplinary approach, a deep understanding of data technologies, and a strategic vision to harness the immense potential that Big Data holds. As we delve further into the world of Big Data Analytics, we will explore strategies and solutions to address these challenges and unlock the transformative power of data.

B.   Characteristics of Big Data: Volume, Variety, Velocity, Veracity, Value

In the digital age, where data pervades every facet of our lives, the concept of Big Data has emerged as a pivotal force reshaping industries and driving innovation. Big Data isn't merely a quantitative leap; it represents a qualitative shift in how we perceive, handle, and extract insights from information. At the heart of this transformation lie five fundamental characteristics that define Big Data: Volume, Variety, Velocity, Veracity, and Value. Together, these characteristics paint a vivid portrait of the complexities and opportunities that Big Data presents.

1. **Volume:** Volume is perhaps the most overt and defining trait of Big Data. It signifies the sheer scale of data generated and collected from an array of sources. This data explosion ranges from social media interactions, sensor readings, financial transactions, to logs and records, creating data repositories that can span petabytes, exabytes, or even zettabytes. This immense volume challenges traditional storage and processing systems, necessitating distributed architectures like Hadoop and cloud-based solutions to accommodate, manage, and analyze data at an unprecedented scale.

2. **Variety:** The variety of data in the Big Data landscape is as diverse as the sources that generate it. It encompasses structured data (databases), semi-structured data (XML, JSON), and unstructured data (text, images, videos). Big Data also involves data from social media posts, clickstreams, sensor readings, and more. This diversity demands versatile processing and analysis techniques, as well as tools that can handle different data formats

and structures. Unleashing the potential of Big Data requires the ability to harmonize and integrate disparate data sources for meaningful analysis.

3. **Velocity:** Velocity refers to the rapid rate at which data is generated, collected, and processed. The real-time or near real-time nature of data streams, such as stock market transactions, social media updates, and sensor data, poses unique challenges. Big Data solutions must enable high-speed data ingestion, processing, and analysis to extract timely insights and support informed decision-making. Technologies like complex event processing (CEP) and stream processing frameworks enable organizations to harness the velocity of data.

4. **Veracity:** Veracity deals with the quality and reliability of data. Big Data is often characterized by noise, inaccuracies, and inconsistencies due to its diverse sources and rapid generation. Ensuring data accuracy and reliability is a critical challenge, as decisions based on erroneous data can lead to misleading conclusions and faulty strategies. Data validation, cleaning, and transformation techniques, coupled with advanced analytics, are employed to address the veracity challenge and enhance data trustworthiness.

5. **Value:** The ultimate goal of Big Data is to derive meaningful insights and value from the vast and complex datasets. Value encapsulates the ability to transform raw data into actionable

knowledge that drives informed decision-making, innovation, and competitive advantage. Extracting value from Big Data involves employing advanced analytics, machine learning, and data mining techniques to uncover hidden patterns, trends, and correlations. This value-driven approach enables organizations to optimize processes, enhance customer experiences, and unlock new revenue streams.

In essence, the characteristics of Big Data - Volume, Variety, Velocity, Veracity, and Value - form a quintessential framework for understanding the intricacies and potential of this transformative domain. The challenges posed by these characteristics are met with innovative technologies, methodologies, and strategies that empower organizations to navigate the complexities of Big Data and harness its immense potential to shape the future. As we delve deeper into the world of Big Data Analytics, we will explore how these characteristics interact and influence the strategies used to extract insights and drive meaningful outcomes.

C. Big Data Technologies and Ecosystem

In the landscape of modern data-driven enterprises, the explosion of data has given rise to an intricate ecosystem of technologies, tools, and frameworks collectively known as the Big Data ecosystem. This ecosystem is a symphony of innovation, enabling organizations to capture, store, process, analyze, and visualize vast volumes of data with unparalleled speed and accuracy. Let's dive into the diverse realm of Big Data technologies, exploring the key components that constitute this dynamic ecosystem.

1. Distributed File Systems:

Hadoop Distributed File System (HDFS): HDFS is the backbone of the Big Data ecosystem. It stores massive datasets across commodity hardware clusters, enabling high-throughput data access and fault tolerance. HDFS divides data into blocks and replicates them across nodes for reliability.

Amazon S3 and Google Cloud Storage: Cloud-based storage solutions like Amazon S3 and Google Cloud Storage provide scalable and durable storage for Big Data, making it accessible from anywhere and eliminating the need for physical infrastructure management.

2. Batch Processing:

Apache MapReduce: MapReduce is a programming model and processing framework that enables parallel processing of large datasets across distributed clusters. It forms the core of Hadoop's data processing capabilities.

3. Real-Time Processing:

Apache Spark: Spark is a versatile and lightning-fast data processing engine that supports both batch and real-time data processing. It offers in-memory computation, making it well-suited for iterative algorithms and interactive data analysis.

Apache Flink: Flink is a stream processing framework designed for high-throughput, low-latency, and exactly-once processing of data streams. It supports event-driven applications and complex event processing.

4. NoSQL Databases:

Apache Cassandra: A distributed NoSQL database designed for high availability and scalability. It handles large amounts of data across commodity servers while providing fault tolerance.

MongoDB: A document-oriented NoSQL database that stores data in a flexible, schema-less format. It is well-suited for applications that require dynamic and unstructured data storage.

5. Data Warehousing and Analytics:

Apache Hive: Hive provides a SQL-like query language, HiveQL, for querying and managing large datasets stored in Hadoop. It translates queries into MapReduce or Tez jobs.

Apache Pig: Pig is a platform for analyzing large datasets using a scripting language called Pig Latin. It abstracts the complexities of MapReduce and simplifies data processing tasks.

Amazon Redshift and Google BigQuery: Cloud-based data warehousing solutions that offer high-performance analytics and querying capabilities for massive datasets.

6. Data Visualization and Business Intelligence:

Tableau, Power BI, Qlik: These tools enable interactive data visualization and business intelligence, allowing users to create insightful dashboards and reports from Big Data sources.

7. Machine Learning and Deep Learning:

Apache Mahout: A library of scalable machine learning algorithms that run on top of Hadoop. It supports clustering, classification, recommendation, and more.

TensorFlow, PyTorch: Widely-used open-source libraries for machine learning and deep learning, enabling the development of complex models for tasks like image recognition and natural language processing.

8. Data Integration and ETL:

Apache NiFi: A data integration and dataflow automation tool that provides a visual interface for designing data pipelines.

Apache Kafka: A distributed event streaming platform that serves as a messaging system for real-time data feeds and processing.

9. **Cloud Services:**

Amazon Web Services (AWS), Google Cloud Platform (GCP), Microsoft Azure: Cloud providers offer a suite of services for storage, computing, analytics, and machine learning, providing scalable and cost-effective solutions for Big Data needs.

10. **Data Governance and Security:**

Apache Ranger: A framework for centralized security administration and authorization across the Hadoop ecosystem.

These are just a few examples within the vast Big Data ecosystem. The convergence of these technologies empowers organizations to navigate the complexities of data at scale, enabling them to transform raw information into actionable insights, innovative solutions, and informed decision-making. As Big Data technologies continue to evolve, this ecosystem will expand and diversify, driving further advancements and propelling the data-driven revolution into new frontiers.

Chapter 3

Data Acquisition and Preprocessing

In the realm of data science and analytics, the journey from raw data to actionable insights begins with the pivotal stages of data acquisition and preprocessing. These stages serve as the foundation upon which the entire data-driven narrative is built. Data acquisition involves the art of collecting diverse and often vast datasets from myriad sources, while preprocessing is the meticulous process of refining, cleaning, and shaping this raw material into a structured and reliable form. This chapter embarks on an exploration of the intricate dance between data acquisition and preprocessing, unveiling the methodologies, challenges, and techniques that lay the groundwork for meaningful analysis. As we delve into the intricacies of these crucial stages, we discover how the quality and integrity of data, acquired and refined with precision, become the bedrock upon which the edifice of accurate insights and impactful decisions stands.

A. Data Collection and Sources

In the age of information, data is the lifeblood that courses through the veins of modern enterprises and fuels the engines of innovation. Data collection, the first critical phase of the data journey, sets the stage for the entire data science and analytics process. It involves gathering, sourcing, and curating data from a multitude of diverse and often complex sources. The effectiveness of data collection influences the quality, relevance, and reliability of subsequent analyses, making it a cornerstone of informed decision-making and transformative insights.

Types of Data Sources:

1.   **Structured Sources**: Structured data originates from well-defined databases, spreadsheets, and data warehouses. It conforms to a rigid schema, making it organized and easily analyzable. Examples include SQL databases, ERP systems, and CRM software.

2.   **Unstructured Sources:** Unstructured data lacks a predefined structure and includes text, images, audio, and video files. Social media posts, emails, and customer reviews are common examples. Analyzing unstructured data often requires specialized techniques like natural language processing (NLP) and computer vision.

3.   **Semi-Structured Sources:** Semi-structured data lies between structured and unstructured. It has some organizational elements, often in the form of tags or labels. JSON and XML files are common semi-structured formats.

4.   **Sensor and IoT Data:** The proliferation of sensors and IoT devices generates real-time data streams. These devices

collect data from the physical world, capturing environmental conditions, machine performance, and more.

5.   **Web Scraping:** Web scraping involves extracting data from websites. It enables organizations to gather information from various online sources, including news articles, product prices, and social media platforms.

6.   **Surveys and Questionnaires:** Organizations often design surveys and questionnaires to collect specific data directly from individuals. This can provide insights into customer preferences, employee satisfaction, and more.

7.   **Public Datasets:** Various organizations and institutions make datasets publicly available for research and analysis. These datasets cover a wide range of topics and can be invaluable for exploratory analysis.

8.   **Internal Data:** Organizations possess a wealth of internal data generated through their daily operations. Sales records, transaction histories, and customer interactions are examples of internal data sources.

Data Collection Challenges:

1.   **Data Quality and Accuracy:** Ensuring the accuracy and quality of collected data is paramount. Inaccurate or incomplete data can lead to misleading conclusions and faulty

decisions.

2.   **Data Privacy and Compliance:** Collecting data must adhere to legal and ethical guidelines, such as GDPR, HIPAA, and industry-specific regulations. Protecting user privacy and maintaining data security are critical considerations.

3.   **Data Volume and Scalability:** Managing and storing large volumes of data requires scalable infrastructure and storage solutions. Cloud services offer scalability to accommodate varying data loads.

4.   **Data Integration:** Combining data from different sources with varying formats and structures can be challenging. Data integration tools and ETL (Extract, Transform, Load) processes are used to harmonize data.

5.   **Real-Time Data Streams:** Collecting and processing real-time data streams from IoT devices and sensors requires robust and efficient data pipelines.

Best Practices in Data Collection:

1.   **Define Clear Objectives:** Start with a clear understanding of the goals and objectives of data collection. Define the specific data points needed to answer key questions.

2.   **Data Governance:** Establish data governance practices to ensure data accuracy, consistency, and compliance

with regulations.

3.   **Automate Collection Processes:** Utilize automation tools for data collection to reduce manual effort and minimize errors.

4.   **Validate and Clean Data:** Implement validation checks and data cleaning processes to address errors and inconsistencies.

5.   **Maintain Documentation:** Document data collection methods, sources, and any transformations applied. Clear documentation ensures transparency and reproducibility.

6.   **Data Sampling:** When dealing with large datasets, consider using data sampling techniques to work with manageable subsets for initial analysis.

As the gateway to the world of data-driven insights, data collection serves as the crucial first step in the data science journey. Successful data collection hinges on a combination of strategic planning, ethical considerations, technical expertise, and meticulous attention to detail. By mastering the art of data collection, organizations pave the way for accurate, meaningful, and transformative analyses that drive innovation and shape the future.

B. Data Cleaning and Transformation

In the intricate tapestry of data science, where raw data is the thread that weaves insights, data cleaning and transformation stand as the loom that shapes the fabric of accurate and meaningful analysis. These essential processes, often referred to as data preprocessing, are the alchemical arts of refining, correcting, and reshaping data to unveil its true potential. As data arrives from diverse sources with imperfections and irregularities, data cleaning and transformation emerge as the unsung heroes that ensure data integrity, enhance analysis quality, and enable confident decision-making.

Data Cleaning:

Data cleaning is the meticulous process of identifying and rectifying errors, inconsistencies, and inaccuracies in a dataset. It is a prerequisite for reliable analysis, as flawed data can lead to erroneous insights and misguided conclusions. The steps involved in data cleaning encompass:

1. **Missing Values Handling:** Missing data can skew analysis and modeling. Techniques like imputation (replacing missing values with estimated ones) or removal of rows or columns with excessive missing data ensure the dataset's integrity.

2. **Outlier Detection and Treatment:** Outliers, data points significantly different from others, can distort analysis

results. Detection methods like Z-score or IQR (Interquartile Range) help identify and handle outliers appropriately.

3.   **Data Standardization:** Standardizing data units, formats, and scales ensures consistency. This is particularly important when merging or comparing data from different sources.

4.   **Data Validation and Integrity Checks:** Ensuring data accuracy through validation rules, such as checking for valid date formats, numerical ranges, or categorical values.

5.   **Deduplication:** Removing duplicate records prevents redundancy and ensures each data point is represented only once.

Data Transformation:

Data transformation involves altering the structure or format of data to make it suitable for analysis or modeling. This process helps uncover patterns, relationships, and insights that might be hidden in the original form. Key transformations include:

1.   **Feature Scaling:** Scaling numerical features to a common range prevents attributes with larger values from dominating the analysis. Techniques like min-max scaling and z-score normalization are commonly used.

2.   **Encoding Categorical Variables:** Many machine learning algorithms require numerical input. Categorical variables

are transformed into numerical representations using techniques like one-hot encoding or label encoding.

3.　　**Feature Extraction:** Creating new features from existing ones can enhance the dataset's predictive power. Principal Component Analysis (PCA) and feature engineering techniques are employed to extract relevant information.

4.　　**Text and NLP Preprocessing:** Text data requires specific transformations like tokenization, stop-word removal, and stemming or lemmatization for meaningful analysis.

5.　　**Date and Time Transformations:** Extracting relevant information from date and time data, such as day of the week or time of day, can uncover temporal patterns.

6.　　**Aggregation and Grouping:** Aggregating and grouping data based on certain attributes can provide summarized insights, such as calculating averages, totals, or frequencies.

Importance of Data Cleaning and Transformation:

1.　　**Data Quality:** Clean and transformed data ensures the accuracy and reliability of analyses and models, leading to more trustworthy insights.

2.　　**Enhanced Analysis:** Properly cleaned and transformed data brings forth hidden patterns and relationships, enhancing the effectiveness of analytical techniques.

3.   **Reduced Bias and Errors:** Data preprocessing mitigates bias introduced by errors or outliers, preventing skewed results and flawed decisions.

4.   **Compatibility:** Transformed data is compatible with various algorithms and models, facilitating the seamless implementation of advanced techniques.

5.   **Effective Visualization:** Well-preprocessed data lends itself to clearer and more insightful data visualizations, aiding communication of findings.

6.   **Time and Resource Efficiency:** Proper data cleaning and transformation reduce the time and effort required for subsequent analysis, modeling, and interpretation.

In the grand symphony of data analysis, data cleaning and transformation compose the harmonious overture that sets the stage for insightful exploration. These processes are the chisels that sculpt raw data into a polished masterpiece, revealing the intricate nuances and hidden gems within. With data cleaned and transformed to its optimal state, data scientists can embark on a journey of discovery, confident in the accuracy, validity, and transformative power of the insights they will uncover.

C. Data Integration and Quality Assurance

In the intricate landscape of data science and analytics, where insights are sought amidst a mosaic of information, the processes of data integration and quality assurance emerge as the cornerstones of reliable decision-making and impactful analysis. Data integration entails the harmonious orchestration of diverse data sources, while quality assurance ensures the accuracy, consistency, and reliability of the amalgamated dataset. Together, these processes transform disparate data fragments into a unified symphony of insights, empowering organizations to extract meaningful patterns, make informed choices, and navigate the complexities of the data-driven world.

Data Integration:

Data integration is the art of merging data from heterogeneous sources into a cohesive and unified format. It encompasses the fusion of structured, semi-structured, and unstructured data, enabling a comprehensive view that transcends the boundaries of individual datasets. This process serves as a bridge between various data silos, unlocking a holistic understanding of relationships, trends, and correlations.

Challenges in Data Integration:

1.   **Diverse Data Formats:** Different sources often use varied data formats, such as databases, spreadsheets, APIs, and logs, requiring transformation for seamless integration.

2.   **Data Consistency:** Ensuring uniformity in data units,

scales, and definitions is essential to avoid discrepancies and misinterpretations.

3.   **Schema Mismatch:** Merging datasets with incompatible schemas can lead to data loss or inaccuracies. Schema mapping and transformation are crucial for alignment.

4.   **Data Redundancy:** Integrating data from multiple sources can lead to redundancy. Effective integration involves identifying and eliminating duplicate information.

5.   **Real-Time Integration:** For applications requiring real-time insights, integrating and processing data streams from diverse sources in real time is challenging but essential.

Data Quality Assurance:

Data quality assurance (QA) is a systematic process that guarantees data accuracy, completeness, and reliability. It involves a series of practices and checks to ensure that the integrated dataset is error-free and fit for analysis. By mitigating errors and inconsistencies, data QA enhances the trustworthiness and credibility of analysis outcomes.

Key Aspects of Data Quality Assurance:

1.   **Data Validation:** Verifying data accuracy by validating against predefined rules and constraints. This ensures that data conforms to expected formats, ranges, and values.

2.   **Data Cleaning:** Cleaning involves identifying and correcting errors, inconsistencies, and missing values. Techniques like outlier removal, imputation, and deduplication are used.

3.   **Data Profiling:** Profiling examines the structure and content of data to uncover anomalies, patterns, and relationships that may require attention.

4.   **Data Enrichment:** Enhancing data by adding relevant external information, such as geolocation data, can enrich analysis outcomes.

5.   **Data Lineage and Audit:** Tracking the origin, transformations, and changes made to data ensures transparency and aids in troubleshooting.

Importance of Data Integration and Quality Assurance:

1.   **Holistic Insights:** Integrated data offers a comprehensive view, enabling a deeper understanding of complex relationships and trends.

2.   **Accurate Decisions:** Quality-assured data ensures that insights and decisions are based on reliable information, minimizing the risk of faulty conclusions.

3.   **Data Trustworthiness:** Effective QA instills confidence in data, fostering trust among stakeholders and users.

4.   **Efficient Operations:** Integrated and quality-assured data streamlines processes, reduces errors, and improves operational efficiency.

5.   **Effective Communication:** High-quality, integrated data enhances communication by providing a consistent and accurate basis for reporting and visualization.

6.   **Regulatory Compliance:** QA ensures compliance with data regulations and industry standards, safeguarding against legal and ethical issues.

In the intricate dance of data integration and quality assurance, disparate data sources are woven together into a cohesive narrative that empowers organizations with insights that drive innovation and growth. By masterfully orchestrating the integration of diverse data streams and meticulously ensuring their quality and accuracy, data professionals illuminate the path to informed decisions, strategic initiatives, and a data-driven future.

Part II

Data Exploration and Analysis

CHAPTER 4

Exploratory Data Analysis (EDA)

In the captivating journey of unraveling the stories hidden within data, Exploratory Data Analysis (EDA) emerges as both compass and compass bearer. EDA is the art of immersion, a preliminary phase where data scientists and analysts dive into the depths of raw data, seeking to comprehend its nuances, unveil patterns, and uncover the seeds of insight. Like an archaeologist meticulously sifting through ancient artifacts, EDA unfurls a narrative of data's past and present, offering a glimpse into its potential future. As we embark on this voyage, we navigate through visualizations, statistics, and intuition, transforming data from mere numbers into a captivating tale that informs decisions, inspires hypotheses, and sets the stage for deeper analytical exploration. EDA is the gateway to understanding, the foundational step that illuminates the path to discovery in the boundless landscape of data analysis.

A. Visualizing and Summarizing Data

In the realm of data analysis, numbers and statistics tell a story, but visualizations and summaries breathe life into that story, making it accessible, comprehensible, and actionable. Visualizing and summarizing data are the twin pillars that bridge the gap between raw data and insightful understanding. They empower data scientists, analysts, and stakeholders to perceive patterns, relationships, and trends that might otherwise remain obscured. By transforming complex datasets into intuitive visuals and concise summaries, these techniques provide a lens through which the richness of data can be explored, interpreted, and harnessed for informed decision-making.

Importance of Visualizations and Summaries:

1.   **Enhancing Perception:** Visualizations provide a visual context that engages human perception more effectively than raw numbers. They enable quick comprehension and aid in spotting trends or anomalies.

2.   **Storytelling:** Visualizations and summaries encapsulate the essence of data, allowing analysts to craft compelling narratives that communicate insights to diverse audiences.

3.   **Hypothesis Generation:** Visual exploration often leads to the formulation of hypotheses, guiding further analysis and investigation.

4.   **Pattern Recognition:** Visualizations facilitate the identification of patterns, correlations, and clusters that might otherwise remain hidden.

5.   **Data Quality Assessment:** Summaries help identify data anomalies or errors by providing an overview of distributions, ranges, and frequencies.

6.   **Decision-Making:** Intuitive visuals empower stakeholders to make informed decisions based on a clear understanding of data insights.

Visualizing Data:

1.   **Bar Charts and Histograms:** Bar charts display categorical data, while histograms depict the distribution of continuous variables.

2.   **Line Charts:** Line charts illustrate trends and changes over time or another continuous variable.

3.   **Scatter Plots:** Scatter plots reveal relationships between two variables, helping to identify correlations or outliers.

4.   **Box Plots:** Box plots provide a compact way to visualize data distributions, including median, quartiles, and potential outliers.

5.   **Heatmaps:** Heatmaps display data matrices using color gradients, making them suitable for displaying correlations or matrices.

6.   **Pie Charts:** Pie charts represent parts of a whole and

are useful for illustrating proportions.

7.   **Geospatial Visualizations:** Maps and geographic visualizations represent data in the context of geographical locations, aiding in spatial analysis.

Summarizing Data:

1.   **Descriptive Statistics:** Metrics like mean, median, mode, standard deviation, and range summarize central tendencies and variability in data.

2.   **Percentiles and Quartiles:** These provide insights into the distribution of data and help identify extreme values.

3.   **Cross-Tabulations:** Cross-tabulating categorical variables provides a summary of how variables interact and influence each other.

4.   **Frequency Tables:** Frequency tables display the count or percentage of occurrences of categorical variables.

5.   **Summary Tables:** Summary tables aggregate data and present key statistics for different subgroups or categories.

6.   **Measures of Association:** Measures like correlation coefficients quantify relationships between variables.

7.   **Data Profiling Reports:** Comprehensive data profiling generates summary statistics and identifies data

anomalies, patterns, and potential issues.

Best Practices for Effective Visualization and Summarization:

1. **Choose Appropriate Visuals:** Select visualizations that best represent the data and insights you want to convey. Avoid using inappropriate or misleading charts.

2. **Simplicity and Clarity:** Keep visuals and summaries simple and easy to interpret. Avoid clutter and unnecessary complexity.

3. **Use Labels and Legends:** Clearly label axes, titles, and legends to ensure viewers understand the context of the visualization.

4. **Interactivity:** Interactive visualizations allow users to explore data from different angles, enhancing engagement and insight discovery.

5. **Consistency:** Maintain consistent formats and scales to enable accurate comparisons across visuals.

6. **Contextualization:** Provide context and explanations to guide viewers' understanding of the data and its implications.

Visualizing and summarizing data are integral steps in the data analysis process, transforming raw information into meaningful insights that drive understanding and decision-making. These techniques empower data professionals to unlock the potential of data, transforming it into a powerful tool for unraveling mysteries, formulating hypotheses, and guiding strategies that shape the future.

B. Detecting Patterns and Anomalies

In the intricate dance of data analysis, the steps of detecting patterns and anomalies are the choreography that reveals the underlying rhythms and deviations within datasets. These steps are the art of discerning order from chaos, uncovering regularities that illuminate insights and identifying aberrations that beckon further investigation. Detecting patterns and anomalies is the heartbeat of exploratory data analysis, a journey that transcends raw numbers and charts to unveil the hidden narratives and anomalies that lie beneath the surface. These processes play a pivotal role in understanding data, making informed decisions, and driving innovation across diverse domains.

Detecting Patterns:

Detecting patterns involves identifying recurring trends, relationships, or structures within data. These patterns can provide valuable insights into underlying mechanisms, behaviors, and dependencies. Recognizing patterns is a blend of art and science, requiring a keen eye for detail, domain expertise, and statistical techniques.

Common Techniques for Detecting Patterns:

1.   **Visual Inspection:** Visualizations like line charts, scatter plots, and heatmaps can reveal trends, cycles, and relationships.

2.   **Time Series Analysis:** Time-dependent data can be analyzed using techniques like moving averages, exponential smoothing, and seasonality decomposition.

3.   **Correlation Analysis:** Quantifying relationships between variables using correlation coefficients helps identify strong associations.

4.   **Cluster Analysis:** Grouping similar data points into clusters helps uncover natural divisions within the dataset.

5.   **Principal Component Analysis (PCA):** PCA identifies patterns by transforming correlated variables into a set of uncorrelated variables (principal components).

6.   **Frequent Pattern Mining:** This technique identifies sets of items that often occur together in transactional data, such as market basket analysis.

Detecting Anomalies:

Anomalies, also known as outliers or exceptions, are data

points that significantly deviate from the norm or expected behavior. Detecting anomalies is vital for ensuring data quality, identifying errors, and uncovering potentially critical events or behaviors.

Techniques for Detecting Anomalies:

1. **Statistical Methods:** Methods like the Z-score or modified Z-score identify data points that deviate significantly from the mean.

2. **Box Plots:** Box plots provide a visual representation of data distribution, highlighting outliers beyond certain thresholds.

3. **Cluster-Based Anomaly Detection:** Anomalies often appear as outliers in clusters. Detecting anomalies involves identifying points far from cluster centers.

4. **Density-Based Anomaly Detection:** This approach identifies regions of lower data density, where anomalies are more likely to reside.

5. **Machine Learning:** Algorithms like Isolation Forest, One-Class SVM, and Autoencoders can learn patterns in normal data and identify anomalies.

6. **Time Series Anomaly Detection:** Time-dependent data can be analyzed using techniques like moving average-based anomaly detection or LSTM-based models.

Challenges in Detecting Patterns and Anomalies:

1.   **Data Complexity:** Complex datasets may contain subtle patterns that are challenging to identify, or anomalies that blend with normal behavior.

2.   **Domain Knowledge:** Understanding the context and domain-specific nuances is crucial for effective pattern detection and anomaly identification.

3.   **Noise and Variability:** Noise and variability in data can obscure true patterns or lead to false alarms in anomaly detection.

4.   **Class Imbalance:** Anomalies are often rare events, leading to class imbalance in anomaly detection tasks.

5.   **Threshold Selection:** Setting appropriate thresholds for pattern detection and anomaly identification requires careful consideration.

Applications:

1.   **Fraud Detection:** Identifying unusual transactions or behaviors in financial data to detect fraudulent activities.

2.   **Quality Control:** Detecting defects or anomalies in manufacturing processes to ensure product quality.

3.   **Healthcare Monitoring:** Identifying abnormal patient

conditions or trends in medical data for early intervention.

4.   **Network Security:** Detecting abnormal network traffic patterns to identify potential cyber threats.

5.   **Predictive Maintenance:** Monitoring equipment sensor data to detect anomalies and predict equipment failures.

Detecting patterns and anomalies transforms data analysis into a voyage of discovery, unveiling insights and irregularities that drive understanding and action. By mastering these techniques, data professionals empower themselves to unveil the stories hidden within data, shape strategies, and contribute to a world where anomalies are opportunities and patterns are pathways to innovation.

C. Feature Engineering and Selection

In the realm of data science and machine learning, where algorithms learn from data to make predictions and decisions, the art of feature engineering and selection is akin to crafting the perfect symphony for a receptive audience. These processes involve sculpting and refining the raw materials of data, transforming them into harmonious melodies that resonate with the algorithms' ability to discern patterns and relationships. Feature engineering and selection are the virtuoso techniques that elevate the performance of models, enhance predictive accuracy, and illuminate the intrinsic structure within data. These practices blend domain knowledge, creativity, and algorithmic finesse to empower models to make informed decisions and drive data-driven innovation.

Feature Engineering:

Feature engineering is the creative process of selecting, transforming, and creating variables (features) from raw data to improve the performance of machine learning models. Effective feature engineering leverages domain expertise and insights to capture relevant information, making it more accessible to algorithms. Well-engineered features enable models to better capture underlying patterns, relationships, and complexities within the data.

Techniques and Strategies in Feature Engineering:

1. **Domain Knowledge:** Understanding the domain and context of the problem at hand is essential for identifying relevant features.

2. **Feature Transformation:** Transforming variables, such as scaling, log-transformations, and power transformations, to ensure they adhere to model assumptions.

3. **Aggregation:** Creating aggregate features by summarizing data across categories, time intervals, or other relevant dimensions.

4.   **Binning and Discretization:** Grouping continuous variables into discrete bins to capture non-linear relationships or reduce noise.

5.   **One-Hot Encoding:** Converting categorical variables into binary vectors to make them suitable for machine learning algorithms.

6.   **Interaction Features:** Creating new features by combining existing ones, capturing interactions between variables.

7.   **Time-Based Features:** Extracting relevant temporal information from date and time data, such as day of the week or time of day.

8.   **Textual Feature Engineering:** Extracting features from text data, such as term frequency-inverse document frequency (TF-IDF) or word embeddings.

Feature Selection:

Feature selection is the process of identifying the most relevant and informative subset of features from the available set. It aims to improve model performance, reduce computational complexity, and mitigate the risk of overfitting, where a model learns noise in the data rather than true patterns.

Methods for Feature Selection:

1.   **Filter Methods:** These methods assess the relevance of features independently of the model. Common metrics include correlation, mutual information, and chi-squared tests.

2.   **Wrapper Methods:** Wrapper methods evaluate subsets of features by training and testing the model iteratively. Techniques like recursive feature elimination (RFE) and forward/backward selection fall under this category.

3.   **Embedded Methods:** These methods incorporate feature selection within the model's training process. Regularization techniques like LASSO (L1 regularization) and decision tree-based methods are examples.

Importance of Feature Engineering and Selection:

1.   **Improved Model Performance:** Well-engineered features enhance the model's ability to capture patterns, leading to better predictive accuracy.

2.   **Dimensionality Reduction:** Effective feature selection reduces the dimensionality of the data, making models more computationally efficient and reducing overfitting.

3.   **Interpretability:** Carefully selected and engineered features improve model interpretability by highlighting the most relevant information.

4.   **Resource Efficiency:** Reducing the number of features can lead to faster training times and reduced memory usage.

5.   **Generalization:** Feature engineering and selection contribute to models that generalize well to unseen data, improving their real-world applicability.

6.   **Domain Understanding:** These practices enable data scientists to gain deeper insights into the relationships between features and the target variable.

Feature engineering and selection are the conductor's baton that guides machine learning models to orchestrate accurate predictions and meaningful insights. By skillfully crafting features and sculpting the input space, data professionals harmonize data and algorithms, transforming raw data into an exquisite performance that resonates with the audience's quest for understanding, innovation, and progress.

CHAPTER 5

Statistical Analysis and Hypothesis Testing

In the realm of data exploration and empirical inquiry, statistical analysis and hypothesis testing stand as the guiding compasses that lead data scientists through the labyrinth of uncertainty. These methodologies provide the means to uncover truth within data, to discern whether observed patterns are mere chance or robust evidence, and to make informed decisions that echo the whispers of probability. Statistical analysis paints a portrait of data's intrinsic properties, while hypothesis testing lends rigor to the quest for understanding, enabling us to challenge assumptions and draw meaningful conclusions. Together, these techniques form the cornerstone of data-driven reasoning, inviting us to peer beneath the surface, scrutinize patterns, and distill significance from complexity in our unending pursuit of knowledge.

A. Descriptive and Inferential Statistics

In the tapestry of data analysis, statistics are the threads that weave the narrative of understanding and insight. Descriptive and inferential statistics are two fundamental branches of this art, each serving distinct yet interconnected roles in unraveling the story hidden within data. Descriptive statistics provide a snapshot of data's essential characteristics, while inferential statistics propel us beyond the immediate observations, enabling us to make broader conclusions and predictions about the world from which the data was sampled.

Descriptive Statistics:

Descriptive statistics are the preliminary brushstrokes that paint a vivid picture of data's basic properties. They summarize and describe data in ways that are both informative and digestible, distilling complex datasets into key measures that provide a snapshot of the underlying distribution, central tendency, variability, and shape. These statistics offer an initial glimpse into the data's landscape, enabling us to uncover patterns and trends and providing a foundation for deeper analysis.

Key Descriptive Statistics:

1.   **Measures of Central Tendency:** These statistics, including the mean, median, and mode, reveal the typical or central value of a dataset.

2.   **Measures of Dispersion:** Variability is encapsulated by measures like the range, variance, and standard deviation, illustrating how spread out the data is.

3.   **Percentiles and Quartiles:** These markers divide the data into segments, providing insights into relative positions and

distributions.

4.   **Skewness and Kurtosis:** These statistics unveil the asymmetry and peakedness of data distributions, offering insights into their shape.

5.   **Frequency Distributions:** Histograms, frequency tables, and density plots portray data distribution patterns.

Inferential Statistics:

While descriptive statistics provide a glimpse into the present, inferential statistics open the door to the future. They extend beyond the observed dataset, allowing us to draw conclusions and make predictions about a larger population from which the data was sampled. Inferential statistics harness the power of probability and hypothesis testing to make educated judgments, enabling us to assess the significance of relationships, differences, and patterns observed in the data.

Key Concepts in Inferential Statistics:

1.   **Sampling and Population:** Inferential statistics involve drawing conclusions about a population based on a representative sample.

2.   **Hypothesis Testing:** Hypothesis testing assesses whether observed differences or effects are statistically significant or merely due to chance.

3.   **Confidence Intervals:** Confidence intervals provide a range of values within which a population parameter is likely to fall.

4.   **Significance Testing:** Significance tests determine whether an observed effect is statistically significant, indicating that it's unlikely to have occurred by random chance.

5.   **P-values:** P-values quantify the strength of evidence against the null hypothesis in hypothesis testing.

6.   **Type I and Type II Errors:** These errors are associated with incorrectly accepting or rejecting a null hypothesis in hypothesis testing.

Importance of Descriptive and Inferential Statistics:

1.   **Understanding Data:** Descriptive statistics provide a foundational understanding of data, revealing its distribution and properties.

2.   **Decision-Making:** Inferential statistics empower informed decision-making by quantifying uncertainty and assessing the strength of evidence.

3.   **Predictive Power:** Inferential techniques allow us to make predictions and draw conclusions about populations beyond the sample.

4.   **Scientific Inquiry:** Statistics are a cornerstone of scientific research, enabling researchers to test hypotheses and draw valid conclusions.

5.   **Communication:** These techniques facilitate clear communication of findings by summarizing and validating insights.

6.   **Quality Assurance**: Descriptive and inferential statistics help identify anomalies, errors, and patterns in data, contributing to data quality.

Descriptive and inferential statistics are the compass and the telescope, guiding data scientists through the labyrinth of information and enabling them to peer beyond the observable into the realm of probability and inference. Armed with these techniques, analysts unveil the hidden tales within data, transforming numbers into knowledge and paving the path to evidence-based discovery and enlightened decision-making.

B. Probability Distributions and Confidence Intervals

In the realm of uncertainty and variability, probability distributions and confidence intervals are the mathematical tools that illuminate the hidden landscapes of chance, guiding data scientists through the enigmatic terrain of randomness. These concepts provide the means to quantify uncertainty, make informed predictions, and draw confident conclusions from data. Probability distributions define the rules of chance that govern random events, while confidence intervals provide a window into the range of likely values for a population parameter. Together, they empower analysts to navigate the seas of uncertainty, extract meaning from data, and embark on a journey of confident discovery.

Probability Distributions:

Probability distributions are the blueprints of randomness, outlining the likelihood of various outcomes in a random process. They underpin statistical analyses, enabling us to quantify the uncertainty associated with data and make probabilistic predictions. Different types of probability distributions exist, each tailored to specific scenarios and types of data.

Key Probability Distributions:

1.   **Normal (Gaussian) Distribution:** This bell-shaped curve is central to many statistical methods, representing a wide range of naturally occurring phenomena.

2.   **Binomial Distribution:** Models the probability of a certain number of successes in a fixed number of independent Bernoulli trials.

3.   **Poisson Distribution:** Describes the probability of a

given number of events occurring in a fixed interval of time or space.

4.   **Exponential Distribution:** Models the time between events in a Poisson process, often used in survival analysis.

5.   **Uniform Distribution:** Represents outcomes that are equally likely within a defined range.

6.   **Gamma Distribution:** Generalizes the exponential distribution to handle non-integer shape parameters.

Confidence Intervals:

Confidence intervals are the safety nets that guard against the precipice of uncertainty, providing a range of values within which a population parameter is likely to lie. These intervals express the precision and reliability of estimates derived from sample data. A confidence interval is typically represented as an interval estimate with a specified confidence level, often 95%, indicating the probability that the true parameter lies within the interval.

Constructing Confidence Intervals:

1.   **Sample Statistics:** The sample mean and standard deviation serve as the foundation for constructing confidence intervals.

2.   **Confidence Level:** The desired level of confidence

(e.g., 95%) determines the width of the interval.

3.   **Standard Error:** The standard error of the sample statistic quantifies the variability of the estimate.

4.   **Z-Score or T-Score:** The appropriate critical value from the standard normal (Z) or t-distribution defines the interval boundaries.

5.   **Margin of Error:** The critical value multiplied by the standard error yields the margin of error, determining the width of the interval.

Interpretation and Use:

1.   **Estimation:** Confidence intervals provide a range of plausible values for a population parameter, aiding in estimation.

2.   **Hypothesis Testing:** Confidence intervals are often used in hypothesis testing to determine if a parameter falls within a certain range.

3.   **Comparative Analysis:** Confidence intervals enable comparisons between groups or populations, assessing whether their parameters differ significantly.

4.   **Prediction:** Confidence intervals are used to predict future values or outcomes based on observed data.

5.   **Communicating Results:** These intervals convey the

precision of estimates and the level of uncertainty to stakeholders.

Importance:

1.   **Quantifying Uncertainty:** Probability distributions and confidence intervals provide a rigorous framework for quantifying and managing uncertainty in data analysis.

2.   **Informed Decision-Making:** Confidence intervals guide decision-makers by offering a range of plausible values for parameters.

3.   **Risk Assessment:** Probability distributions allow us to assess and mitigate risks associated with uncertain outcomes.

4.   **Scientific Inquiry:** These concepts underpin scientific research, allowing researchers to draw valid conclusions from sample data.

Probability distributions and confidence intervals are the cornerstones of probabilistic reasoning, enabling analysts to navigate the seas of chance with clarity and confidence. Armed with these tools, data scientists unlock the doors to probabilistic insights, predictions, and decisions, casting light on the unknown and empowering exploration in the realm of uncertainty.

C. A/B Testing and Experimental Design

In the realm of data-driven decision-making, A/B testing and experimental design are the architects of controlled exploration, the methodologies that allow us to sift through variables, isolate effects, and illuminate causal relationships. These techniques serve as the crucibles of empirical inquiry, enabling researchers and analysts to discern the impact of interventions, treatments, or changes in a controlled and systematic manner. A/B testing, often referred to as split testing, is a specific application of experimental design that compares two or more variants to determine their impact on a chosen outcome. Together, A/B testing and experimental design guide the pursuit of truth, empowering us to make informed choices, optimize processes, and drive innovation with evidence-based insights.

Experimental Design:

Experimental design is the blueprint for scientific investigation, guiding the orchestration of experiments to systematically assess the effects of variables. It involves careful planning, randomization, and control to minimize biases and confounding factors that could distort results. Proper experimental design ensures that conclusions drawn from the experiment can be confidently attributed to the variables being tested.

Key Components of Experimental Design:

1.   **Research Question:** Clearly defining the research question or hypothesis to be tested is the starting point of experimental design.

2.   **Control and Treatment Groups:** Assigning subjects or samples to control and treatment groups ensures a valid comparison between different conditions.

3.   **Randomization:** Randomly assigning subjects to groups minimizes the risk of bias and ensures groups are comparable.

4.   **Replication:** Conducting the experiment multiple times increases the reliability of results and allows for the assessment of variability.

5.   **Blinding:** Single-blind or double-blind methods prevent participants or researchers from being influenced by knowledge of the experimental conditions.

6.   **Covariate Control:** Accounting for covariates (variables that might influence the outcome) through statistical methods enhances the validity of the experiment.

A/B Testing:

A/B testing is a specialized form of experimental design commonly used in marketing, product development, and web optimization. It involves comparing two or more variants of a treatment, often denoted as A and B, to evaluate their impact on a predefined outcome. A/B testing allows organizations to make data-driven decisions by directly measuring the effects of changes on user behavior, conversions, or other key performance metrics.

Steps in A/B Testing:

1.   **Hypothesis Formulation:** Clearly define the hypothesis to be tested and the specific outcome metrics to be measured.

2.   **Variant Design:** Create different variants (A and B) that represent the changes or interventions to be tested.

3.   **Random Assignment:** Randomly assign users or samples to the A and B groups to ensure a fair comparison.

4.   **Data Collection:** Collect data on user interactions or outcomes for each variant during the experiment.

5.   **Statistical Analysis:** Apply statistical techniques to compare the performance of variants and determine if observed differences are statistically significant.

6.   **Inference and Conclusion:** Based on the analysis, draw conclusions about the impact of the changes and make informed decisions.

Importance and Applications:

1.   **Data-Driven Decision-Making:** Experimental design and A/B testing provide objective evidence for making decisions and optimizing strategies.

2. **Product Optimization:** A/B testing helps optimize product features, user interfaces, and user experiences.

3. **Marketing Campaigns:** A/B testing informs the effectiveness of marketing strategies, such as ad copy, visuals, and targeting.

4. **Website Optimization:** A/B testing is used to improve website conversion rates, user engagement, and user journeys.

5. **Process Improvement:** Experimental design aids in identifying process improvements, such as changes in manufacturing methods or operational procedures.

6. **Scientific Research:** Experimental design is fundamental in scientific research for testing hypotheses and establishing causal relationships.

A/B testing and experimental design are the scientific lenses that allow us to peer into the intricacies of cause and effect. These methodologies enable us to dissect complex systems, untangle webs of variables, and reveal the underlying mechanisms that govern the world around us. Armed with the principles of controlled experimentation, data professionals harness the power to shape strategies, refine products, and push the boundaries of knowledge, all guided by the empirical illumination offered by A/B testing and experimental design.

CHAPTER 6

Machine Learning for Predictive Modeling

In the age of data-driven insights, where patterns lie beneath the surface of information and predictions hold the keys to informed decisions, machine learning emerges as the beacon that transforms data into foresight. Machine learning for predictive modeling is the art and science of building algorithms that learn from data to make accurate predictions or classifications. It's a journey into the realm of algorithms that uncover hidden relationships, discover trends, and forecast future outcomes with remarkable precision. As data becomes the fuel and algorithms the engines, machine learning equips us with the tools to navigate uncertainty, transform information into knowledge, and embark on a voyage of discovery that reshapes industries, informs strategies, and advances our understanding of the world.

A. Regression and Classification Algorithms

In the symphony of machine learning, regression and classification algorithms are the virtuoso performers that harmonize data and models, orchestrating predictions and decisions that span diverse domains. These algorithms form the bedrock of supervised learning, where data-driven patterns are extracted from labeled examples to guide future predictions. Regression predicts continuous numerical values, while classification assigns data points to predefined categories. Together, they empower machines to mimic human cognitive processes, capturing the essence of relationships and making informed judgments with computational finesse.

Regression Algorithms:

Regression algorithms are the architects of continuous prediction, mapping input features to output values on a continuous scale. They analyze the relationships between variables to model and predict numerical outcomes. Regression plays a crucial role in tasks like sales forecasting, price prediction, and trend analysis.

Key Regression Algorithms:

1.   **Linear Regression:** The simplest form, linear regression models the relationship between input features and the target variable using a linear equation.

2.   **Polynomial Regression:** Extending linear regression, this algorithm accommodates non-linear relationships by incorporating polynomial terms.

3.   **Ridge and Lasso Regression:** Regularization techniques that prevent overfitting by penalizing large

coefficients.

4.   **Support Vector Regression:** Based on support vector machines, this algorithm predicts continuous values while minimizing prediction errors.

5.   **Decision Tree Regression:** Hierarchical tree structures split data into subsets based on feature thresholds, predicting the average of target values within each subset.

6.   **Random Forest Regression:** An ensemble method combining multiple decision trees to improve predictive accuracy and robustness.

Classification Algorithms:

Classification algorithms are the detectives of categories, deciphering data points and assigning them to predefined classes or labels. They're foundational for tasks such as image recognition, spam detection, sentiment analysis, and medical diagnoses.

Key Classification Algorithms:

1.   **Logistic Regression:** Despite its name, logistic regression is a classification algorithm that estimates the probability of belonging to a particular class.

2.   **K-Nearest Neighbors (KNN):** KNN assigns a label to

a data point based on the labels of its nearest neighbors in the feature space.

3.   **Decision Trees:** Decision trees partition data into categories by asking a series of binary questions, forming a tree-like structure.

4.   **Random Forest Classification:** Similar to its regression counterpart, random forest classification creates an ensemble of decision trees to enhance accuracy.

5.   **Support Vector Machines (SVM):** SVM finds the optimal hyperplane that best separates classes in a high-dimensional feature space.

6.   **Naive Bayes:** Based on Bayes' theorem, naive Bayes assumes feature independence and calculates conditional probabilities to classify data.

7.   **Neural Networks:** Deep learning models comprising interconnected layers that learn hierarchical representations for complex classification tasks.

Challenges and Considerations:

1.   **Overfitting**: Both regression and classification models can overfit, learning noise instead of patterns. Regularization techniques help mitigate this.

2.   **Feature Selection:** Choosing relevant features is crucial for model performance and interpretability.

3.   **Imbalanced Data:** In classification, imbalanced class distributions can lead to biased models. Techniques like oversampling and undersampling address this.

4.   **Hyperparameter   Tuning:**   Optimizing hyperparameters enhances model performance and generalization.

5.   **Interpretability:** While some algorithms, like linear regression, offer interpretability, others, like neural networks, are less transparent.

Applications:

1.   **Regression Applications:** Sales forecasting, real estate price prediction, stock market analysis, temperature prediction, demand forecasting.

2.   **Classification Applications:** Image classification, sentiment analysis, email spam detection, disease diagnosis, fraud detection.

Regression and classification algorithms are the maestros that translate data into decisions, capturing the symphony of patterns and relationships that shape our world. These algorithms stand as the bridge between data and insight, between information and action, guiding machines to wield predictive power and aiding humans in navigating complexities, making informed choices, and unraveling the mysteries that lie within data.

B. Model Selection and Evaluation Metrics

In the realm of machine learning, where algorithms vie for the throne of predictive prowess, model selection and evaluation metrics act as the judges that assess their merits and guide us toward the most effective choices. These critical components of the data-driven journey determine the success of a machine learning endeavor, steering us toward models that best capture underlying patterns and generalization. Model selection involves choosing the right algorithm or architecture, while evaluation metrics quantify a model's performance and provide actionable insights for refinement. Together, they form the compass that navigates the complex landscape of model development, enabling us to build robust, accurate, and impactful machine learning solutions.

Model Selection:

Model selection is the art of finding the algorithm or model architecture that best fits the data and the problem at hand. It involves a careful balance between simplicity and complexity, avoiding overfitting (fitting noise) or underfitting (oversimplification). The goal is to strike the optimal trade-off between capturing patterns in the training data and generalizing well to new, unseen data.

Considerations in Model Selection:

1.   **Problem Type:** Different algorithms are suited for regression, classification, clustering, and other tasks. Understanding the problem type is essential.

2.   **Data Size:** Large datasets may benefit from more complex models, while smaller datasets might require simpler models to avoid overfitting.

3.   **Feature Complexity:** Complex relationships may require models that can capture non-linear patterns, such as decision trees or neural networks.

4.   **Interpretability:** Some models, like linear regression, offer transparency and interpretability, while others, like deep neural networks, are more opaque.

5.   **Computational Resources:** Some algorithms are computationally expensive, which may influence the choice of model.

6.   **Domain Expertise:** Knowledge of the problem domain can guide the selection of models that align with known relationships.

Evaluation Metrics:

Evaluation metrics are the measuring sticks that quantify a model's performance and effectiveness. They provide tangible insights into how well a model is achieving its objectives and allow for comparisons between different models. The choice of evaluation metric depends on the specific problem and the desired outcome.

Key Evaluation Metrics:

1.   **Regression Metrics:** Mean Squared Error (MSE), Root Mean Squared Error (RMSE), Mean Absolute Error (MAE), R-squared (Coefficient of Determination).

2.   **Classification Metrics:** Accuracy, Precision, Recall (Sensitivity), F1-score, Area Under the Receiver Operating Characteristic Curve (AUC-ROC).

3.   **Clustering Metrics:** Silhouette Score, Davies-Bouldin Index, Calinski-Harabasz Index.

4.   **Ranking Metrics:** Mean Average Precision (MAP), Normalized Discounted Cumulative Gain (NDCG).

Model Evaluation Workflow:

1.   **Training and Validation:** Split data into training and validation sets for model development and tuning.

2.   **Hyperparameter Tuning:** Adjust hyperparameters to optimize model performance using techniques like grid search or random search.

3.   **Cross-Validation:** Perform k-fold cross-validation to assess model generalization by training and validating on different subsets of data.

4.   **Evaluate on Test Set:** Test the final model on a separate, unseen test dataset to estimate its real-world performance.

5.   Interpretation and Comparison: Analyze evaluation metrics to understand a model's strengths, weaknesses, and comparative performance.

Importance and Impact:

1.   **Effective Decision-Making:** Model selection and evaluation metrics guide informed choices that align with project goals.

2.   **Optimized Performance:** Rigorous model evaluation ensures that the selected model performs well on unseen data.

3.   **Resource Efficiency:** Proper model selection avoids wasting resources on overly complex or inappropriate models.

4.   **Solution Improvement:** Evaluation metrics highlight

areas for improvement and guide iterative model refinement.

5.   **Domain Understanding:** Metrics provide insights into the behavior of models in specific contexts, aiding in domain-specific decision-making.

Model selection and evaluation metrics are the navigational tools that chart the course to effective machine learning solutions. Armed with a deep understanding of problem domains and the wisdom of evaluation metrics, data practitioners steer models toward accuracy, robustness, and utility, sculpting algorithms that wield predictive power and drive data-driven insights.

C. Model Interpretability and Explainability

In the era of complex machine learning algorithms and intricate deep neural networks, the demand for model interpretability and explainability shines as a beacon of transparency and accountability. As machine learning becomes increasingly integrated into decision-making processes across industries, the need to understand and trust these models has become paramount. Model interpretability and explainability encompass the techniques and methods that unveil the inner workings of black-box algorithms, demystifying their decision-making processes and shedding light on the factors that drive their predictions. These principles not only foster trust and compliance but also empower humans to collaborate effectively with machines, understand the implications of decisions, and pave the path to responsible and ethical AI deployment.

Model Interpretability:

Model interpretability refers to the ability to understand and make sense of a model's predictions, insights, and internal mechanisms. It involves converting complex mathematical representations into human-understandable forms without compromising a model's predictive performance.

Methods for Model Interpretability:

1.   **Feature Importance:** Techniques like permutation importance, SHAP (SHapley Additive exPlanations), and LIME (Local Interpretable Model-agnostic Explanations) assign importance scores to input features, revealing their impact on predictions.

2.   **Partial Dependence Plots (PDPs):** PDPs illustrate how a feature's values influence predictions while keeping other features constant.

3.   **Global vs. Local Interpretability:** Global methods offer insights into a model's behavior across the entire dataset, while local methods focus on understanding individual predictions.

4.   **Decision Trees and Rule-based Models**: These

inherently interpretable models provide explicit decision paths and conditions for predictions.

5.   **Linear Regression Coefficients:** In linear models, coefficient values indicate the direction and magnitude of feature contributions.

6.   **Attention Mechanisms:** Common in deep learning, attention mechanisms highlight relevant parts of the input data that the model focused on.

Model Explainability:

Model explainability delves deeper by providing insights into why a model made a specific decision. It answers questions such as, "Why was this particular prediction made?" and "What features drove this outcome?"

Methods for Model Explainability:

1.   **Local Explanations:** LIME generates interpretable explanations for individual predictions by fitting a simple, interpretable model locally.

2.   **Feature Importance Explanations:** SHAP values provide a unified framework for explaining the output of any machine learning model based on feature contributions.

3.   **Counterfactual Explanations:** These hypothetical

scenarios show how changes to input features could result in different model predictions.

4.   **Saliency Maps:** Common in image analysis, saliency maps highlight the pixels that contributed most to a model's decision.

5.   **Feature Attribution:** Capturing the contribution of each feature to the final prediction, often visualized through heatmaps or overlays.

Importance and Impact:

1.   **Trust and Accountability:** Interpretable and explainable models foster trust by revealing the rationale behind predictions, helping users understand and accept outcomes.

2.   **Ethical AI:** Transparency and accountability are crucial for identifying and addressing biases, ensuring fair and ethical decision-making.

3.   **Regulatory Compliance:** In industries like healthcare and finance, regulatory authorities often require models to be interpretable and explainable.

4.   **Human-Machine Collaboration:** Interpretability enables humans to collaborate effectively with AI, making joint decisions and refining models.

5.   **Debugging and Diagnosis:** Interpretable models aid in diagnosing issues, identifying erroneous predictions, and improving model robustness.

6.   **Education and Communication:** Interpretable explanations bridge the gap between technical experts and stakeholders, facilitating effective communication.

Model interpretability and explainability elevate machine learning from enigmatic black boxes to transparent decision-making tools. By unveiling the inner mechanisms, motivations, and rationales behind predictions, these principles bridge the gap between data science and human understanding. They empower us to navigate the complex landscape of machine learning with clarity, responsibility, and the assurance that decisions are guided by knowledge, insight, and accountability.

Part III

Big Data Technologies and Tools

CHAPTER 7

Big Data Storage and Processing

In the digital age, where data proliferates at an unprecedented pace, the realm of big data storage and processing emerges as the bedrock of modern information management. As the volume, velocity, variety, and veracity of data escalate to monumental proportions, traditional approaches prove inadequate. Big data storage and processing stand as the architectural marvels that tame the data deluge, providing the infrastructure and frameworks to store, manage, and derive value from vast and diverse datasets. From distributed file systems to real-time processing, this domain unlocks the potential of big data, enabling organizations to transform raw information into actionable insights, innovation, and informed decision-making.

A. Distributed File Systems: HDFS and S3

In the landscape of big data storage and processing, distributed file systems play a pivotal role in managing and harnessing the power of massive datasets. Two prominent names in this domain are the Hadoop Distributed File System (HDFS) and Amazon Simple Storage Service (S3). These distributed file systems address the challenges posed by storing and accessing vast amounts of data, offering scalable, fault-tolerant, and efficient solutions that underpin the infrastructure of modern data-driven applications and analytics.

Hadoop Distributed File System (HDFS):

HDFS is the cornerstone of the Apache Hadoop ecosystem, designed specifically to handle the storage and processing of large datasets across clusters of commodity hardware. HDFS follows a distributed architecture, dividing files into smaller blocks and replicating them across multiple nodes to ensure data availability and fault tolerance.

Key Features and Concepts of HDFS:

1.   **Data Replication:** HDFS replicates data blocks across nodes in the cluster to ensure high availability. The default replication factor is configurable.

2.   **Block Size:** HDFS breaks files into fixed-size blocks (typically 128 MB or 256 MB) for efficient storage and processing.

3.   **Master-Slave Architecture:** HDFS consists of two main components: the NameNode (master) that manages metadata and DataNodes (slaves) that store data blocks.

4.   **Data Locality:** HDFS aims to optimize data locality by processing data on nodes where it's stored, reducing network

traffic.

5.   **High Throughput:** HDFS is optimized for batch processing and is well-suited for applications with large-scale data processing needs.

6.   **Write-Once, Read-Many (WORM):** Once data is written to HDFS, it is rarely modified, aligning with the batch processing paradigm.

Amazon Simple Storage Service (S3):

Amazon S3, part of Amazon Web Services (AWS), is a highly scalable and durable object storage service designed to store and retrieve vast amounts of data. S3 is not limited to Hadoop clusters and can be used independently to store a wide variety of data types, including files, images, videos, and backups.

Key Features and Concepts of S3:

1.   **Object Storage:** S3 uses a flat object storage model, where each object consists of data, metadata, and a unique identifier.

2.   **Scalability:** S3 can handle virtually unlimited amounts of data, accommodating both small and large organizations' storage needs.

3.   **Durability and Availability:** S3 offers high durability

by replicating data across multiple availability zones within a region, ensuring data resilience.

4.   **Data Consistency:** S3 provides strong read-after-write consistency for newly uploaded objects and eventual consistency for overwrite operations.

5.   **Access Control:** S3 offers granular access control using bucket policies, Access Control Lists (ACLs), and AWS Identity and Access Management (IAM) roles.

6.   **Data Lifecycle Management:** S3 supports automatic data archiving, tiering, and deletion based on user-defined policies.

Comparison:

1.   **Data Types:** HDFS is optimized for storing and processing large volumes of structured and unstructured data, while S3 is a versatile object storage solution suitable for various data types.

2.   **Access Patterns:** HDFS is well-suited for batch processing and analytics, whereas S3 is designed for general-purpose storage and supports use cases like content delivery and backups.

3.   **Deployment:** HDFS is commonly used in Hadoop clusters deployed on-premises or in the cloud, while S3 is a cloud-

native storage service offered by AWS.

4.   **Consistency:** HDFS provides strong consistency within the cluster, while S3 offers eventual consistency across multiple availability zones.

5.   **Management and Maintenance:** HDFS requires cluster management, including hardware, software, and fault tolerance. S3 abstracts the underlying infrastructure, simplifying management.

In summary, HDFS and S3 are two prominent distributed file systems that address the challenges of big data storage and processing. HDFS is tightly integrated with the Hadoop ecosystem and excels in batch processing, while S3 offers versatile object storage suitable for various use cases within the AWS environment. Choosing between the two depends on factors such as deployment architecture, data processing requirements, and overall infrastructure strategy.

B. Batch Processing with MapReduce

In the realm of big data processing, batch processing using the MapReduce paradigm stands as a cornerstone, enabling the efficient analysis of massive datasets. Conceived by Google and popularized by the Apache Hadoop project, MapReduce provides a framework for processing vast amounts of data in parallel across distributed clusters. This paradigm is particularly well-suited for offline processing, where data is processed in bulk, leading to insights, aggregations, and transformations that drive decision-making and business intelligence.

Key Components of MapReduce:

1.   **Map Function:** The map function takes a set of input data, processes each element, and produces a set of key-value pairs as intermediate outputs.

2.   **Shuffling and Sorting:** The MapReduce framework automatically groups and sorts the intermediate key-value pairs based on keys, preparing them for the reduce phase.

3.   **Reduce Function:** The reduce function aggregates and processes the grouped key-value pairs, producing the final output.

MapReduce Workflow:

1.   **Input Splitting:** The input data is divided into smaller splits, which are processed independently by map tasks running on multiple nodes in the cluster.

2.   **Mapping:** The map tasks process the input splits, applying the map function to each record and generating intermediate key-value pairs.

3.   **Shuffling and Sorting:** The framework groups and

sorts the intermediate key-value pairs based on keys, preparing them for the reduce phase.

4.　　**Reducing:** The reduce tasks process the grouped data, applying the reduce function to perform aggregations or computations.

5.　　**Output:** The final output is written to the distributed file system, typically HDFS, making it available for further analysis or consumption.

Advantages of MapReduce:

1.　　**Scalability:** MapReduce inherently scales horizontally by distributing tasks across a cluster of nodes, enabling efficient processing of large datasets.

2.　　**Fault Tolerance:** MapReduce ensures fault tolerance by automatically reassigning tasks to healthy nodes in case of failures.

3.　　**Parallelism:** The parallel execution of map and reduce tasks maximizes the utilization of resources, reducing processing time.

4.　　**Simplicity:** MapReduce abstracts the complexity of distributed processing, allowing developers to focus on logic rather than infrastructure.

Limitations of MapReduce:

1.   **Batch Processing:** MapReduce is designed for batch processing and may not be suitable for real-time or interactive applications.

2.   **Data Movement:** Shuffling data during the shuffle and sort phase can lead to high network traffic and performance bottlenecks.

3.   **Complexity:** While abstracting distributed processing, MapReduce programming can still be complex, especially for intricate tasks.

Use Cases:

1.   **Log Analysis:** Extracting insights from log files to understand user behavior and system performance.

2.   **Data Aggregation:** Summarizing and aggregating data for reporting, analytics, and business intelligence.

3.   **ETL (Extract, Transform, Load):** Preparing and transforming raw data before loading it into a data warehouse or database.

4.   **Data Cleansing:** Cleaning and processing data to remove duplicates, errors, and inconsistencies.

5.   **Text Analysis:** Analyzing large volumes of text data

for sentiment analysis, topic modeling, and natural language processing.

Modern Alternatives and Evolution:

While MapReduce revolutionized big data processing, modern data processing frameworks like Apache Spark have emerged to address its limitations. Spark offers in-memory processing, real-time streaming, and more advanced APIs, making it suitable for a broader range of use cases, including batch processing. Nevertheless, MapReduce remains a foundational concept that paved the way for the big data revolution, leaving an indelible mark on the world of data engineering and analytics.

C. Real-Time Processing with Apache Spark

In the era of dynamic and time-sensitive data, traditional batch processing may fall short in meeting the demands of real-time insights and rapid decision-making. Apache Spark, a versatile and high-performance data processing framework, rises to the occasion, offering a comprehensive solution for real-time processing, streaming analytics, and interactive queries. Born out of the need for speed and agility, Spark's real-time capabilities empower organizations to process and analyze data streams as they arrive, enabling timely responses, actionable insights, and enhanced user experiences.

Real-Time Processing in Spark:

Real-time processing in Spark is facilitated through its streaming module, known as Spark Streaming. This module provides an abstraction for processing live data streams in mini-batches, making it appear similar to batch processing. However, Spark Streaming processes data in small, fixed time intervals, allowing for near real-time processing with low-latency.

Key Concepts of Spark Streaming:

1. **DStream (Discretized Stream):** DStream is the fundamental data structure in Spark Streaming, representing a continuous stream of data divided into small batches.

2. **Micro-Batching:** Spark Streaming processes data in micro-batches, typically ranging from a few milliseconds to seconds, ensuring low-latency processing.

3. **Transformation and Output Operations:** Similar to batch processing in Spark, DStreams support various transformations and output operations for data manipulation and analysis.

4. **Windowed Operations:** Windowed operations allow processing data over a sliding window of time, enabling computations on specific time intervals.

5. **Sources and Sinks:** Spark Streaming supports various

sources (e.g., Kafka, Flume, HDFS, sockets) to ingest data and sinks (e.g., HDFS, databases) to store processed results.

Advantages of Real-Time Processing with Spark:

1. **Low Latency:** Spark Streaming's micro-batching approach enables low-latency processing, making it suitable for real-time use cases.

2. **Unified Platform:** Spark provides a unified platform for batch, interactive, and streaming processing, simplifying development and maintenance.

3. **Fault Tolerance:** Spark Streaming offers fault tolerance through lineage information, enabling recovery in case of node failures.

4. **Scalability:** The scalability of Spark's distributed computing model extends to Spark Streaming, accommodating growing data volumes.

5. **Ease of Use:** Developers familiar with Spark's batch processing APIs can easily transition to Spark Streaming, reducing the learning curve.

Use Cases of Real-Time Processing with Spark:

1. **Fraud Detection:** Detecting anomalies and fraudulent activities in real-time financial transactions.

2.   **Social Media Analysis:** Monitoring and analyzing social media streams for trending topics, sentiment analysis, and brand perception.

3.   **IoT Data Processing:** Analyzing data from Internet of Things (IoT) devices in real time for predictive maintenance and performance optimization.

4.   **Network Monitoring:** Real-time analysis of network logs for security threats, intrusion detection, and traffic optimization.

5.   **E-commerce   Personalization:**   Real-time recommendations for online shoppers based on browsing and purchase behavior.

Challenges and Considerations:

1.   **Data Ordering:** Ensuring the correct order of data arrival in micro-batches is crucial for maintaining data integrity.

2.   **State Management:** Managing stateful computations in real-time processing can be complex and requires careful design.

3.   **Data Drift:** Dealing with changing data distributions and concepts over time is a challenge in real-time analytics.

Future Directions:

As the demand for real-time insights continues to grow, Apache Spark evolves to meet emerging challenges. Spark's Structured Streaming, introduced in later versions, aims to provide even more seamless integration between batch and real-time processing by unifying batch and streaming APIs. This evolution reflects Spark's commitment to enabling efficient and agile real-time data processing, making it a valuable asset in the modern data engineering toolbox.

CHAPTER 8

NoSQL and Big Data Databases

In the ever-expanding landscape of data management, traditional relational databases have found themselves challenged by the demands of the digital age. The rise of massive datasets, diverse data types, and the need for agile, scalable solutions has given birth to a new class of databases known as NoSQL (Not Only SQL) databases. These databases are designed to handle the complexities of big data, providing flexible data models, horizontal scalability, and improved performance. NoSQL databases have become a cornerstone of modern data management, offering a versatile set of options to store, retrieve, and process data in ways that challenge the conventions of traditional relational databases. This evolution brings forth a new paradigm in database technology, one that embraces the diversity and volume of data characteristic of the big data era.

A. Types of NoSQL Databases: Document, Columnar, Key-Value, Graph

As the volume, variety, and velocity of data continue to surge, the limitations of traditional relational databases have paved the way for a diverse landscape of NoSQL (Not Only SQL) databases.

NoSQL databases are purpose-built to handle the complexities of modern data, offering flexible data models, horizontal scalability, and efficient storage and retrieval. Within the NoSQL realm, four primary types of databases have emerged: Document, Columnar, Key-Value, and Graph databases. Each type addresses specific data management challenges and excels in different use cases, collectively reshaping how data is stored, managed, and analyzed.

Document Databases:

Document databases are designed to store and manage semi-structured or unstructured data in flexible, JSON-like documents. Each document can have varying structures, making these databases suitable for applications where data schemas may evolve over time.

Key Features:

1.   **Schema Flexibility:** Documents within a collection can have different structures, accommodating changes without affecting the entire database.

2.   **Complex Data:** Document databases handle nested data structures and arrays, making them ideal for data with varying depths.

3.   **Scalability:** Many document databases support horizontal scaling, distributing data across multiple nodes for

improved performance.

Use Cases: Content management systems, e-commerce catalogs, blogging platforms, user profiles, and real-time analytics.

Examples: MongoDB, Couchbase, RavenDB.

Columnar Databases:

Columnar databases store data in columns rather than rows, optimizing data storage and retrieval for analytics and reporting. They excel in scenarios where aggregation and analytical queries are frequent.

Key Features:

1.   **Column Storage:** Data is organized in columnar format, allowing for efficient compression, improved query performance, and selective reading.

2.   **Analytics:** Columnar databases are optimized for analytical workloads, enabling fast query execution on large datasets.

3.   **Aggregation:** These databases excel in aggregating and summarizing data for reporting and data analysis.

Use Cases: Business intelligence, data warehousing, time-series data analysis, log analysis, and large-scale reporting.

Examples: Apache Cassandra, Apache HBase, Amazon Redshift.

Key-Value Databases:

Key-Value databases store data as pairs of keys and associated values, making them simple and efficient for basic data storage and retrieval. They are particularly suitable for use cases that require fast and predictable data access.

Key Features:

1.   **Simplicity:** Key-Value databases offer straightforward data storage and retrieval with minimal overhead.

2.   **Speed:** These databases provide fast read and write operations, making them ideal for caching and real-time applications.

3.   **Scalability:** Key-Value databases can be distributed across multiple nodes, providing scalability for large datasets.

Use Cases: Caching, session management, user profiles, real-time applications, and high-velocity data scenarios.

Examples: Redis, Amazon DynamoDB, Riak.

Graph Databases:

Graph databases are optimized for managing and querying

relationships between data entities. They excel at traversing complex networks and revealing insights hidden within connected data.

Key Features:

1.   **Graph Structure:** Data is stored as nodes (entities) and edges (relationships), facilitating efficient relationship traversal.

2.   **Relationship Centric:** Graph databases are designed to express and navigate relationships, making them valuable for social networks, recommendation systems, and fraud detection.

3.   **Complex Queries:** These databases excel in querying and analyzing complex relationship patterns.

Use Cases: Social networks, recommendation engines, fraud detection, knowledge graphs, and network analysis.

Examples: Neo4j, Amazon Neptune, ArangoDB.

Choosing the Right NoSQL Database:

Selecting the appropriate NoSQL database type depends on the nature of your data, the use case requirements, and your performance and scalability needs. Each database type offers unique features and trade-offs, allowing organizations to tailor their data management solutions to match their specific challenges and goals. As the NoSQL landscape continues to evolve, these diverse database types collectively provide the foundation for modern data management in the big data era.

B. Using NoSQL Databases for Big Data Applications

In the landscape of data-driven applications, the convergence of big data and NoSQL databases has ushered in a new era of data management, enabling organizations to efficiently handle vast volumes of diverse and rapidly changing data. NoSQL databases, with their flexible data models, horizontal scalability, and performance optimizations, have become essential tools for building and deploying big data applications. These databases empower businesses to extract value from their data, make informed decisions, and deliver seamless user experiences in the face of the ever-expanding data landscape.

Advantages of Using NoSQL Databases for Big Data:

1.   **Flexible Schema:** NoSQL databases accommodate unstructured, semi-structured, and evolving data schemas, enabling businesses to ingest and process data without rigid constraints.

2.   **Scalability:** NoSQL databases offer horizontal scalability, allowing organizations to handle increasing data volumes by distributing data across clusters of nodes.

3.   **High Performance:** NoSQL databases are optimized for specific data access patterns, leading to efficient read and write operations, making them well-suited for high-velocity data.

4.   **Real-Time Processing:** NoSQL databases, particularly document and key-value databases, facilitate real-time processing and quick responses, crucial for applications demanding low latency.

5.   **Complex Relationships:** Graph databases excel in representing and querying complex relationships, critical for applications involving network analysis, recommendation systems, and knowledge graphs.

Use Cases of NoSQL Databases in Big Data Applications:

1.   **Internet of Things (IoT):** NoSQL databases handle the massive data influx from IoT devices, allowing real-time ingestion, analysis, and visualization of sensor data.

2.   **Social Media Analytics:** Document and graph databases enable the storage and analysis of social network data, facilitating sentiment analysis, trend detection, and influencer identification.

3.   **E-Commerce:** NoSQL databases power personalized product recommendations, inventory management, and order processing in real time.

4.   **Healthcare:** NoSQL databases manage and analyze electronic health records, medical images, and patient data for predictive analytics and patient care.

5.   **Gaming:** Real-time player interactions, leaderboards, and in-game events benefit from NoSQL databases' low-latency data storage and retrieval.

6.   **Financial Services:** NoSQL databases process and analyze vast transaction datasets, detect fraud patterns, and provide real-time insights for trading and risk management.

Challenges and Considerations:

1.   **Data Modeling:** While NoSQL databases provide flexibility, designing an appropriate data model is essential to ensure efficient data access and query performance.

2.   **Consistency and Transactions:** Some NoSQL databases prioritize availability over strong consistency, necessitating careful design to handle data consistency in distributed systems.

3.   **Tooling and Expertise:** Adopting NoSQL databases may require training and expertise in the specific database technology and related tools.

4.   **Data Migration:** Migrating from traditional databases to NoSQL databases may involve data transformation and

migration challenges.

Selecting the Right NoSQL Database:

Choosing the right NoSQL database for a big data application depends on factors such as data structure, access patterns, scalability requirements, and latency constraints. The various types of NoSQL databases—document, columnar, key-value, and graph—offer distinct advantages and trade-offs, making careful evaluation crucial to ensuring a successful fit for the application's needs.

In Conclusion:

NoSQL databases have revolutionized the way big data is managed and analyzed, providing the agility, scalability, and performance required to meet the challenges of today's data-intensive world. By harnessing the capabilities of NoSQL databases, organizations can unlock the potential of their data, drive innovation, and deliver impactful user experiences in the dynamic landscape of big data applications.

C. Data Modeling and Querying

In the realm of data management, data modeling and querying are fundamental processes that lay the foundation for effective data organization, storage, and retrieval. These processes are pivotal in ensuring data is structured, accessible, and optimized for efficient analysis and decision-making. With the advent of big data and the diversity of NoSQL databases, data modeling and querying have evolved to address new challenges while leveraging the strengths of modern data management technologies.

Data Modeling:

Data modeling is the process of defining the structure, relationships, and constraints of data to represent real-world entities and their interactions. Effective data modeling ensures data accuracy, integrity, and consistency, facilitating organized storage and retrieval.

Key Aspects of Data Modeling:

1. **Entity-Relationship (ER) Modeling:** ER models depict entities (objects, people, concepts) and their relationships, helping to visualize data structure.

2. **Schema Design:** In NoSQL databases, schema design involves defining document structures, column families, or key-value pair formats.

3. **Normalization and Denormalization:** In relational databases, normalization reduces redundancy, while NoSQL databases may involve denormalization for efficient query performance.

4. **Aggregation and Nesting:** Document-oriented

databases allow nesting data structures for better representation of complex relationships.

Querying:

Querying is the process of retrieving specific data from a database using queries, which are structured commands written in a query language. Effective querying ensures that data can be accessed and manipulated according to application requirements.

Key Aspects of Querying:

1. **Query Languages:** SQL (Structured Query Language) is prevalent in relational databases, while NoSQL databases have their query languages or APIs (Application Programming Interfaces).

2. **CRUD Operations:** CRUD (Create, Read, Update, Delete) operations allow inserting, retrieving, updating, and deleting data in databases.

3. **Aggregation and Transformation:** Aggregation functions, joins, and data transformations allow complex analysis and reporting.

4. **Indexes:** Indexes enhance query performance by facilitating quick data retrieval based on specific fields.

Data Modeling and Querying in NoSQL Databases:

In NoSQL databases, data modeling and querying differ from traditional relational databases due to their schema flexibility and diverse data models. Each NoSQL database type has unique considerations:

1. **Document Databases:** Data modeling involves defining document structures in formats like JSON or BSON. Querying often includes filtering, projection, and aggregation operations on nested document fields.

2. **Columnar Databases:** Schema design focuses on defining column families and data types. Querying allows for efficient analysis and aggregation on columnar data.

3. **Key-Value Databases:** Data modeling centers around choosing appropriate keys and associated values. Queries primarily involve retrieving values using keys.

4. **Graph Databases:** Data modeling revolves around defining nodes, edges, and properties to represent relationships. Querying focuses on traversing and analyzing complex graph structures.

Challenges and Considerations:

1. **Flexibility vs. Complexity:** NoSQL databases offer flexibility but require careful data modeling to ensure efficient

querying and analysis.

2.   **Scalability:** Data modeling and querying should consider the scalability requirements of the application and the database technology.

3.   **Performance:** Proper indexing, caching, and query optimization are crucial for achieving good performance.

4.   **Migration and Evolution:** As data evolves, data models and queries may need adaptation, requiring a strategy for data migration and application updates.

Future Directions:

Advancements in machine learning and artificial intelligence are influencing data modeling and querying. Techniques like schema inference, auto-indexing, and query optimization based on machine learning algorithms are becoming prevalent.

In the big data era, where data diversity and volume are paramount, mastering data modeling and querying remains essential. Whether working with traditional relational databases or the diverse landscape of NoSQL databases, these processes are pivotal in unlocking the value hidden within data and driving meaningful insights and innovation.

CHAPTER 9

Data Visualization and Communication

In the age of information overload, data visualization emerges as a powerful tool to transform complex datasets into meaningful insights, aiding comprehension and decision-making. Data visualization goes beyond presenting numbers; it employs graphical elements to convey patterns, trends, and relationships that might otherwise remain obscured. Effective data visualization and communication bridge the gap between data and understanding, enabling professionals to tell compelling stories, unearth insights, and facilitate informed actions. This interdisciplinary field combines aesthetics, design principles, and data analysis to create visual narratives that resonate with audiences across domains and backgrounds.

A. Design Principles for Effective Data Visualization

Effective data visualization goes beyond creating pretty charts; it involves thoughtful design that enhances understanding, communicates insights, and guides decision-making. Whether conveying complex analytics or simplifying intricate patterns, adhering to design principles ensures that visualizations are clear, impactful, and informative. These principles guide the creation of visual narratives that resonate with viewers, making data more accessible and actionable. Here are key design principles for crafting compelling and effective data visualizations:

1. Clarity and Simplicity:

• Keep visualizations simple and uncluttered to avoid overwhelming viewers.

• Use a clear and concise title or caption to communicate the main message.

• Minimize unnecessary elements that distract from the core data insights.

2. Data Integrity and Accuracy:

• Ensure data accuracy and integrity, avoiding misleading representations.

• Choose appropriate scales and axes to accurately reflect data relationships.

• Clearly label data points, axes, and units to prevent misinterpretation.

3. Purposeful Visual Encoding:

• Select appropriate visual encodings (e.g., color, size,

position) to represent data attributes effectively.

• Use consistent and intuitive mapping of data variables to visual properties.

4. Storytelling and Narrative:

• Craft a compelling narrative that guides viewers through the visualization's story.

• Use annotations, captions, and callouts to highlight key insights and context.

5. Context and Relevance:

• Provide contextual information to help viewers understand the data's significance.

• Consider the audience's background and knowledge to tailor the visualization's level of detail.

6. Color and Contrast:

• Use color purposefully to emphasize data points, relationships, or trends.

• Ensure sufficient contrast for readability, especially in labels and text.

7. Data Hierarchy and Focus:

- Emphasize the most important data points by adjusting size, color, or position.

- Use hierarchy to guide viewers' attention from general trends to specific details.

8. Consistency and Standardization:

- Maintain visual consistency across multiple visualizations to aid comparison.

- Use consistent color schemes, fonts, and icons throughout the presentation.

9. Interactive Elements:

- Incorporate interactive features like tooltips, zooming, or filtering to allow viewers to explore the data further.

- Ensure interactivity enhances understanding rather than causing confusion.

10. Accessibility:

- Design visualizations that are accessible to all users, including those with visual impairments.

- Provide alternative text descriptions and consider colorblind-friendly palettes.

11. **Contextualization and Exploration:**

•   Place data in relevant context, such as historical trends or benchmarks, to facilitate meaningful interpretation.

•   Allow viewers to explore different aspects of the data to encourage discovery.

12. **Iteration and Feedback:**

•   Iteratively refine visualizations based on feedback and testing to improve their effectiveness.

•   Seek input from diverse stakeholders to ensure the visualization resonates with various perspectives.

13. **Minimal Chartjunk:**

•   Avoid unnecessary decorations, embellishments, or "chartjunk" that detract from the data's clarity.

14. **Emphasis on Insight, Not Decoration:**

•   Prioritize conveying insights and actionable information over decorative elements.

By adhering to these design principles, data visualizations transform into potent tools that bridge the gap between data and understanding. Effective visualization design enables professionals to communicate complex ideas, uncover patterns, and drive better decision-making, ultimately harnessing the power of data to inform and inspire.

B. Creating Interactive Visualizations

Interactive visualizations represent a dynamic evolution in the field of data communication, enabling users to engage with data in real-time, explore insights, and uncover patterns that might otherwise remain hidden. Interactivity transforms static visuals into immersive experiences, empowering users to tailor their exploration and gain a deeper understanding of complex datasets. Through intuitive interactions, interactive visualizations facilitate storytelling, foster discovery, and enhance decision-making. To create effective interactive visualizations, designers combine data analysis, design aesthetics, and user experience principles, resulting in a powerful tool for conveying information and driving engagement.

Key Aspects of Creating Interactive Visualizations:

1. Data Preparation:

- Begin with clean and well-structured data to ensure accurate and meaningful interactions.

- Perform data transformations, aggregations, and filtering to support dynamic exploration.

2. **Platform and Tools:**

• Choose appropriate tools and libraries for interactive visualization, such as D3.js, Plotly, Tableau, or Power BI.

• Consider the target platform (web, desktop, mobile) and its compatibility with interactive features.

3. **Intuitive Navigation:**

• Provide intuitive navigation controls, such as zooming, panning, and scrolling, to allow users to explore different levels of detail.

4. **Filters and Controls:**

• Include interactive filters, sliders, and dropdowns that enable users to manipulate data dimensions or attributes.

• Allow users to customize the visualization to their preferences and focus on specific aspects.

5. **Tooltips and Hover Effects:**

• Display contextual information and details when users hover over data points, aiding understanding without cluttering the visualization.

6. **Linked Views:**

• Connect multiple visualizations to allow users to

interact with one visualization and observe the effects on others.

- Linked views facilitate holistic exploration of data relationships.

7. Animation and Transitions:

- Use animations and transitions to smoothly reveal changes in data over time or in response to interactions.

- Transitions enhance user engagement and comprehension.

8. Storytelling Sequences:

- Incorporate storytelling elements by guiding users through a sequence of interactive steps, revealing insights progressively.

9. Drill-Down and Drill-Up:

- Implement drill-down and drill-up functionalities to let users explore data at different levels of granularity.

10. Dynamic Dashboards:

- Create dynamic dashboards that combine multiple interactive visualizations on a single screen, allowing users to gain a comprehensive view of the data.

11. **Performance Optimization:**

• Optimize performance to ensure smooth interaction even with large datasets or complex visualizations.

• Implement data aggregation and sampling techniques to enhance responsiveness.

12. **Accessibility:**

• Design with accessibility in mind, ensuring that interactive elements can be navigated and understood by users with disabilities.

13. **User Testing and Feedback:**

• Conduct user testing to gather feedback on the effectiveness of interactive features and identify areas for improvement.

Benefits of Interactive Visualizations:

1. **Engagement:** Interactivity captivates users, encouraging them to explore and spend more time with the data.

2. **Discovery:** Users can uncover patterns, outliers, and trends through personalized exploration.

3. **Contextual Understanding:** Interactive elements provide context and details on demand, enhancing

comprehension.

4.   **Customization:** Users can tailor the visualization to their needs, focusing on specific aspects of interest.

5.   **Collaboration:** Interactive visualizations facilitate collaborative data exploration and discussion among teams.

Challenges and Considerations:

1.   **Usability:** Strive for a balance between interactivity and usability, avoiding overwhelming users with too many options.

2.   **Mobile-Friendly Design:** Ensure that interactive features work smoothly on various devices, including mobile devices with touch interfaces.

3.   **Data Integrity:** Interactivity should not compromise data accuracy; ensure that dynamic changes maintain data consistency.

In Conclusion:

Interactive visualizations are a dynamic tool for conveying complex information, enabling users to actively engage with data and gain meaningful insights. By blending data analysis, design aesthetics, and user experience principles, designers can create interactive visualizations that empower users to explore, discover, and comprehend data on a deeper level. Through thoughtful implementation of interactive features, data communication becomes not just informative, but also interactive and engaging.

C. Storytelling with Data

In the realm of data communication, storytelling with data has emerged as a powerful approach to convey insights, engage audiences, and drive meaningful actions. Beyond presenting raw numbers and charts, storytelling integrates data into a compelling narrative that resonates with viewers, making complex information accessible, relatable, and impactful. By weaving data-driven narratives, storytellers guide audiences through a journey of discovery, enabling them to connect emotionally with data, understand its significance, and make informed decisions. Effective storytelling with data requires a harmonious blend of data analysis, visualization design, and narrative structure to create a cohesive and memorable experience.

Key Elements of Storytelling with Data:

1. **Context and Purpose:**

• Establish the context by outlining the problem, question, or scenario that the data addresses.

• Clearly define the purpose of the story: to inform, persuade, inspire action, or prompt critical thinking.

2. Audience Understanding:

- Consider the audience's background, knowledge, and interests to tailor the story's level of complexity and relevance.

3. Data Exploration and Analysis:

- Thoroughly analyze the data to unearth insights, trends, patterns, and relationships.

- Identify the key messages and insights that align with the story's purpose.

4. Narrative Structure:

- Introduce a compelling narrative structure, including an engaging opening, development of tension, climax, and resolution.

- Use storytelling techniques like anecdotes, metaphors, or real-world examples to make data relatable.

5. Visualization Design:

- Create clear, concise, and aesthetically pleasing visualizations that support the narrative.

- Choose appropriate chart types, color palettes, and visual encodings to enhance understanding.

6. **Flow and Sequence:**

• Organize the story's flow logically, guiding viewers through the data and insights in a coherent manner.

• Use transitions between visualizations and sections to maintain a smooth and engaging experience.

7. **Contextualization:**

• Provide historical, cultural, or industry context to help viewers understand the data's significance and implications.

8. **Emphasis and Hierarchy:**

• Highlight the most important insights or takeaways using emphasis techniques like size, color, or positioning.

9. **Human-Centered Approach:**

• Humanize the data by connecting it to real people, stories, or scenarios, making it more relatable and engaging.

10. **Ethical Considerations:** -

• Ensure data accuracy, integrity, and transparency to build trust with the audience. - Be transparent about data sources, assumptions, and limitations.

11. Call to Action:

- Conclude the story with a clear call to action that aligns with the story's purpose, encouraging viewers to apply the insights.

Benefits of Storytelling with Data:

1. **Engagement:** Storytelling captivates attention and sustains interest, fostering deeper engagement with the data.

2. **Comprehension:** Narratives provide context and structure, facilitating easier comprehension of complex information.

3. **Retention:** Well-crafted stories are more memorable, increasing the likelihood that the data's message will be retained.

4. **Decision-Making:** Effective storytelling guides audiences to draw informed conclusions and make data-driven decisions.

5. **Persuasion:** Storytelling evokes emotional connections, making it an effective tool for persuasion and advocacy.

Challenges and Considerations:

1. **Simplification:** Balancing simplicity with depth is crucial to prevent oversimplification or overwhelming

complexity.

2.   **Data Integrity:** Ensure data accuracy and representativeness to maintain the story's credibility.

3.   **Audience Diversity:** Adapt the storytelling approach to resonate with diverse audiences with varying knowledge levels.

In Conclusion:

Storytelling with data transcends mere information sharing; it transforms data into a narrative that informs, inspires, and influences. By blending data-driven insights with narrative structure, visualization design, and audience understanding, storytellers create a compelling journey that sparks curiosity, triggers emotions, and guides viewers toward meaningful understanding and action. In a world saturated with data, storytelling emerges as a guiding light that illuminates insights and turns numbers into stories worth remembering.

Part IV

Interview Preparation

CHAPTER 10

Excelling in Data Science and Big Data Analytics Interviews

Navigating the interview process in the field of data science and big data analytics requires more than technical prowess; it demands a strategic blend of technical expertise, problem-solving acumen, effective communication, and a deep understanding of the industry's landscape. Excelling in these interviews goes beyond showcasing knowledge; it involves demonstrating your ability to harness data for insightful solutions, collaborate with multidisciplinary teams, and address real-world challenges. Aspiring data professionals must not only master algorithms and coding but also develop a holistic skill set that encompasses analytical thinking, communication finesse, and a knack for ethical decision-making. This chapter delves into the art of preparing for, tackling, and excelling in data science and big data analytics interviews, providing insights to help you shine in a competitive and dynamic field.

A. Understanding Interview Expectations

Interviews for data science and big data analytics roles are a crucial gateway to securing a position in this competitive field. To excel in these interviews, it's essential to not only showcase your technical skills but also demonstrate your ability to solve complex problems, communicate effectively, and contribute to a data-driven environment. Understanding the expectations of these interviews can significantly enhance your preparation and performance.

Technical Proficiency:

Interviewers expect candidates to possess a strong foundation in technical concepts related to data science and big data analytics. This includes:

1.   **Algorithms and Data Structures:** Be prepared to discuss algorithms, data structures, and their applications. Expect questions on sorting, searching, graphs, trees, and more.

2.   **Programming Languages:** Proficiency in languages like Python, R, or SQL is often required. Be ready to write code, analyze code snippets, and explain algorithms.

3.   **Machine Learning and Statistics:** Understand various machine learning algorithms, their assumptions, strengths, and weaknesses. Be able to explain concepts like bias-variance tradeoff, cross-validation, and feature engineering.

4.   **Big Data Technologies:** Familiarity with tools like Hadoop, Spark, and NoSQL databases is crucial for roles involving big data analytics.

Problem-Solving Skills:

Expect to encounter real-world data problems that require creative thinking and analytical reasoning. Interviewers want to see how you approach unfamiliar challenges and break them down into manageable steps. Emphasize your problem-solving process, logical reasoning, and your ability to arrive at practical solutions.

Communication and Storytelling:

Data scientists are expected to effectively communicate their findings to both technical and non-technical audiences. Interviewers may evaluate your ability to explain complex concepts in simple terms. Practice articulating your thought process, summarizing your insights, and structuring your responses in a clear and organized manner.

Domain Knowledge:

Depending on the specific industry or domain of the company, interviewers may assess your familiarity with relevant concepts. For instance, if you're interviewing for a healthcare data science role, understanding medical terminology and healthcare challenges could be beneficial.

Project Experience:

Expect questions about your previous projects, including the problem you tackled, the approach you took, challenges you encountered, and the impact of your solutions. Highlight projects that showcase your technical skills, problem-solving abilities, and your capacity to drive meaningful outcomes.

Cultural Fit and Collaboration:

Employers often seek candidates who can collaborate effectively with cross-functional teams. Be prepared to discuss how you've worked with other departments, shared insights, and contributed to a collaborative work environment.

Ethical Considerations:

Given the sensitive nature of data, interviewers might inquire about your approach to data privacy, bias mitigation, and ethical decision-making. Be ready to discuss how you handle these aspects in your work.

Continuous Learning:

Data science is a rapidly evolving field. Interviewers may ask about your willingness and strategies for staying updated on the latest trends, technologies, and methodologies in the industry.

Preparation Tips:

1.   **Study the Job Description:** Tailor your preparation to match the skills and qualifications mentioned in the job description.

2.   **Practice Problem-Solving:** Solve coding challenges, practice data analysis, and work on case studies to refine your problem-solving skills.

3.   **Behavioral Questions:** Be ready to answer questions about your experiences, teamwork, leadership, and overcoming challenges.

4.   **Mock Interviews:** Conduct mock interviews with peers, mentors, or interview coaches to simulate real interview scenarios.

5.   **Research the Company:** Understand the company's data-driven initiatives, products, and industry to demonstrate your genuine interest.

6.   **Ask Questions:** Prepare thoughtful questions about the company's data projects, team dynamics, and future goals to show your engagement.

By comprehending and aligning with interview expectations, you position yourself as a well-rounded candidate who not only possesses technical proficiency but also possesses the qualities needed to thrive in the dynamic world of data science and big data analytics.

B. Common Technical and Behavioral Questions in Data Science and Big Data Analytics Interviews

Data science and big data analytics interviews often comprise a mix of technical and behavioral questions to assess a candidate's technical proficiency, problem-solving abilities, and interpersonal skills. Preparing for both types of questions is crucial to showcase your expertise and demonstrate your fit for the role and the team. Here's an in-depth look at the types of questions you might encounter:

Technical Questions:

1.   **Coding Challenges:** These questions assess your coding skills, algorithmic thinking, and understanding of data structures. Expect tasks like implementing algorithms, solving puzzles, or writing efficient code.

2.   **Machine Learning Concepts:** Be prepared to explain machine learning algorithms (e.g., linear regression, decision trees, neural networks), evaluation metrics (e.g., accuracy, precision, recall), and concepts like overfitting and underfitting.

3.   **Statistical Analysis:** You might encounter questions about probability, hypothesis testing, confidence intervals, and

experimental design. Be ready to explain concepts like p-values and the Central Limit Theorem.

4.   **Data Manipulation:** Expect questions related to data cleaning, transformation, and feature engineering. You might be asked to deal with missing values, outliers, and normalization.

5.   **SQL Queries:** For roles involving data querying and manipulation, anticipate questions about SQL queries, joins, aggregations, and subqueries.

6.   **Big Data Technologies:** If the role involves big data, you might be questioned about tools like Hadoop, Spark, and NoSQL databases. Expect queries about their use cases and benefits.

7.   **Data Visualization:** Be prepared to discuss best practices for creating effective visualizations, interpreting charts, and choosing appropriate chart types.

8.   **Technical Case Studies:** You might be given a real-world scenario and asked to devise a data-driven solution. Demonstrate your ability to structure your approach, use relevant tools, and communicate your thought process.

Behavioral Questions:

1.   **Tell Me About Yourself:** This open-ended question allows you to introduce yourself and highlight relevant

experiences, skills, and motivations.

2. **Teamwork and Collaboration:** Be ready to share instances when you've worked effectively in teams, resolved conflicts, and contributed to group projects.

3. **Problem-Solving and Adaptability:** Discuss challenges you've faced, how you approached them, and the steps you took to find solutions.

4. **Leadership and Initiative:** Provide examples of times when you've taken the lead, initiated projects, or demonstrated ownership of a task.

5. **Communication Skills:** Showcase your ability to convey complex concepts to non-technical stakeholders. Provide examples of instances where you've communicated technical insights effectively.

6. **Ethical Dilemmas:** You might be asked about ethical considerations related to data privacy, bias, or fairness. Discuss how you approach these challenges.

7. **Time Management:** Explain how you handle multiple tasks, prioritize work, and manage your time effectively.

8. **Learning and Growth:** Share experiences of how you've stayed updated with new technologies and methodologies in the ever-evolving field.

Preparation Strategies:

1.   **Review Fundamentals:** Brush up on core technical concepts, algorithms, and data manipulation techniques.

2.   **Practice Coding:** Solve coding challenges on platforms like LeetCode, HackerRank, or CodeSignal to improve your coding skills.

3.   **Mock Interviews**: Conduct mock interviews to simulate real interview scenarios. Receive feedback to refine your responses.

4.   **Behavioral Examples:** Prepare stories that illustrate your skills in teamwork, problem-solving, leadership, and ethical decision-making.

5.   **Company Research:** Understand the company's values, projects, and culture to tailor your responses accordingly.

6.   **Asking Questions:** Prepare thoughtful questions about the team, projects, and the company's data-driven goals.

By mastering both technical and behavioral questions, you present yourself as a well-rounded candidate who not only possesses the technical skills needed for the role but also fits well within the team and the organization's culture.

C. Effective Communication and Problem-Solving Skills in Data Science and Big Data Analytics

In the dynamic landscape of data science and big data analytics, technical proficiency alone is not enough. Professionals in these fields must excel in both communication and problem-solving to effectively collaborate, innovate, and drive impactful outcomes. Effective communication ensures that insights are understood and actions are taken, while strong problem-solving skills enable the transformation of complex challenges into data-driven solutions. Here's an in-depth exploration of the significance of these skills and how to cultivate them:

Effective Communication:

1. **Interpreting and Explaining Data:** Data scientists must translate complex data insights into clear, concise, and actionable information for non-technical stakeholders. The ability to convey findings, trends, and implications in a way that resonates with various audiences is paramount.

2. **Visualization and Storytelling:** Visualizations are powerful tools for communication. Being able to design compelling visuals and weave them into a coherent narrative helps convey insights and engage audiences effectively.

3. **Collaboration:** Effective collaboration requires clear

communication to bridge gaps between technical and non-technical team members. Data professionals need to listen actively, explain concepts, and foster a culture of knowledge-sharing.

4.   **Documentation:**   Clearly   documenting methodologies, assumptions, and code is essential for replicability and knowledge transfer within the team.

5.   **Presentations:** The ability to present findings in meetings, conferences, and discussions demonstrates confidence, clarity, and an aptitude for engaging an audience.

Cultivating Effective Communication:

1.   **Practice Storytelling:** Craft stories around data, using relatable examples and real-world applications to make your insights memorable.

2.   **Feedback and Adaptation:** Seek feedback on your communication from peers and mentors. Adapt based on their input to continually improve.

3.   **Public Speaking:** Participate in workshops or courses to enhance your public speaking and presentation skills.

4.   **Visual Design:** Familiarize yourself with data visualization best practices and tools to create compelling and informative visuals.

Problem-Solving Skills:

1.   **Analytical Thinking:** Data professionals analyze complex datasets, identify patterns, and derive insights. The ability to break down problems into manageable components and approach them analytically is crucial.

2.   **Creativity:** Data scientists often encounter unique challenges that require creative solutions. Cultivate the ability to think outside the box and explore innovative approaches.

3.   **Hypothesis Generation and Testing:** Formulating hypotheses and testing them using data-driven methods is central to problem-solving in data science.

4.   **Decision-Making:** Use data-driven insights to make informed decisions. Consider trade-offs and evaluate options based on data analysis.

5.   **Iterative Approach:** Problem-solving often involves an iterative process of experimentation, evaluation, and refinement. Embrace this cycle to improve solutions continuously.

Cultivating Problem-Solving Skills:

1.   **Practice Critical Thinking:** Engage in puzzles, brain teasers, and coding challenges to enhance your logical thinking.

2.   **Real-World Projects:** Undertake diverse data projects

that challenge your problem-solving skills and expose you to various scenarios.

3.   **Cross-Disciplinary Learning:** Explore fields outside data science to gain new perspectives and broaden your problem-solving toolkit.

4.   **Mentorship and Collaboration:** Collaborate with experienced professionals to learn problem-solving techniques and strategies.

5.   **Continuous Learning:** Stay updated with emerging methodologies, tools, and approaches to enrich your problem-solving capabilities.

In the intersection of effective communication and problem-solving lies the ability to transform complex data into meaningful insights and actionable solutions. Mastery of these skills not only enhances your technical abilities but also positions you as a valuable asset in any data-driven team or organization, contributing to successful projects and driving innovation.

CHAPTER 11

Technical Interview Preparation

Preparing for technical interviews is a crucial step on the path to a successful career in data science and big data analytics. These interviews evaluate your problem-solving skills, technical knowledge, and ability to apply concepts to real-world scenarios. Technical interview preparation is not only about memorizing algorithms and syntax; it involves honing your analytical thinking, coding proficiency, and confidence in tackling challenging data-related problems. This section delves into the strategies, resources, and mindset needed to excel in technical interviews, guiding you on your journey to becoming a proficient and sought-after data professional.

A. Analyzing Data Science Scenarios and Challenges

In data science technical interviews, candidates are often presented with real-world scenarios and challenges to assess their problem-solving skills, analytical thinking, and ability to apply data science methodologies. These scenarios mirror the complexities data professionals encounter in their roles and require a structured approach to unravel. Navigating these challenges effectively demonstrates your practical knowledge, adaptability, and creativity. Here's an in-depth look at how to analyze data science scenarios and challenges during technical interviews:

Understanding the Problem:

1.   **Read Carefully:** Begin by thoroughly understanding the given scenario or problem statement. Pay attention to details, context, and the specific question you need to address.

2.   **Clarify Assumptions:** If the scenario is ambiguous or lacks certain information, don't hesitate to ask for clarifications or make reasonable assumptions. This demonstrates your critical thinking and ensures you're on the right track.

Identifying the Approach:

1.   **Define the Problem:** Clearly define the problem you're aiming to solve. Break it down into smaller components or sub-tasks to make it more manageable.

2.   **Identify Data:** Determine what data is available and relevant to the problem. Consider the types of data (structured, unstructured), sources, and potential data preprocessing steps required.

3.   **Choose Methodologies:** Based on the problem's nature, decide on appropriate data science methodologies. This

might involve exploratory data analysis, machine learning, statistical analysis, or a combination.

Data Exploration and Analysis:

1.   **Exploratory Data Analysis (EDA):** Perform initial data exploration to understand the data's distribution, patterns, and potential outliers. Visualizations and summary statistics can aid this process.

2.   **Feature Engineering:** If necessary, engineer new features that might enhance the predictive power of your model. This could involve creating interaction terms, transformations, or aggregations.

Modeling and Evaluation:

1.   **Model Selection:** Choose suitable algorithms for the task, considering factors like data size, complexity, and the problem's goals. Justify your selection based on algorithm strengths and the problem's characteristics.

2.   **Training and Validation:** Split the data into training and validation sets. Train your model on the training set, adjusting hyperparameters if needed, and evaluate its performance on the validation set.

3.   **Metrics:** Select appropriate evaluation metrics (accuracy, precision, recall, F1-score, etc.) based on the problem's

requirements. Explain why you chose these metrics and interpret the results.

Iterative Process:

1.   Refinement: If your initial approach doesn't yield satisfactory results, iterate and refine. This might involve experimenting with different algorithms, adjusting parameters, or revisiting data preprocessing.

Communication:

1.   **Narrate Your Thought Process:** As you work through the scenario, explain your thought process aloud. Interviewers value transparency in your thinking, even if you encounter challenges or uncertainties.

2.   **Visualize and Interpret:** Use visualizations, charts, or tables to communicate your findings effectively. Interpret these visuals to extract meaningful insights.

Preparation Strategies:

1.   **Practice Scenarios:** Engage in mock scenarios and challenges to simulate interview conditions and refine your approach.

2.   **Real Projects:** Undertake real-world data projects to gain experience in tackling diverse challenges and applying

methodologies.

3.   **Collaboration:** Discuss and analyze problems with peers or mentors to gain different perspectives and insights.

4.   **Stay Updated:** Stay informed about the latest data science methodologies and tools to broaden your problem-solving toolkit.

By mastering the art of analyzing data science scenarios and challenges, you demonstrate your proficiency in translating theoretical knowledge into practical solutions. This ability showcases your potential to excel in real-world data-driven projects and solidifies your position as a competent data science professional.

B. Designing and Implementing Machine Learning Pipelines

Machine learning pipelines are systematic workflows that encapsulate the end-to-end process of building, training, evaluating, and deploying machine learning models. They play a pivotal role in data science and big data analytics by enabling efficient and reproducible model development. Designing and implementing effective machine learning pipelines requires careful consideration of data preprocessing, feature engineering, model selection, hyperparameter tuning, and deployment strategies. Here's an in-depth exploration of the key components and best practices for designing and implementing machine learning pipelines:

Components of a Machine Learning Pipeline:

1.   Data Collection and Preprocessing:

•   Begin by collecting and cleaning your data. Handle missing values, outliers, and data inconsistencies.

•   Preprocess data through techniques like normalization, scaling, and one-hot encoding.

•   Split data into training, validation, and test sets to ensure unbiased model evaluation.

2.   Feature Engineering:

•   Engineer relevant features from raw data to improve model performance.

•   Create new features, transform variables, and extract meaningful information from text or images.

3.   Model Selection and Training:

•   Choose appropriate algorithms based on the problem type (classification, regression, clustering, etc.) and data characteristics.

•   Train multiple models using the training data, tuning hyperparameters to optimize performance.

4. Model Evaluation:

• Evaluate model performance using appropriate metrics, such as accuracy, precision, recall, or F1-score.

• Employ cross-validation to assess generalization on different subsets of the data.

5. Hyperparameter Tuning:

• Fine-tune model hyperparameters to optimize performance. Techniques like grid search or random search can aid in this process.

6. Ensemble Methods (Optional):

• Combine predictions from multiple models (ensemble methods) to enhance robustness and accuracy.

7. Model Deployment:

• Deploy the trained model in a production environment, making predictions on new, unseen data.

• Implement monitoring mechanisms to track model performance and potential drift over time

Best Practices for Designing and Implementing Pipelines:

1.   Modularity and Reusability:

•   Design your pipeline in a modular fashion, allowing components to be easily swapped or updated.

•   Reuse code and functions to ensure consistency and reduce redundancy.

2.   Automation:

•   Automate repetitive tasks using scripting or tools like Apache Airflow to ensure reproducibility and consistency.

3.   Version Control:

•   Use version control systems (e.g., Git) to track changes in your pipeline and collaborate effectively with team members.

4.   Documentation:

•   Maintain detailed documentation for each step in the pipeline, including preprocessing, model architecture, and hyperparameter choices.

5.   Scalability:

•   Design pipelines that can handle large datasets efficiently and can be scaled horizontally or vertically.

6.   Error Handling and Logging:

• Implement error handling mechanisms and robust logging to diagnose and troubleshoot issues during pipeline execution.

7.   Pipeline Monitoring:

• Continuously monitor the performance of your pipeline, models, and deployed systems. Detect anomalies and ensure timely updates.

Cultural Considerations:

1.   **Collaboration:** Foster collaboration by creating pipelines that are easy for team members to understand, modify, and extend.

2.   **Agility:** Design pipelines that can adapt to changing requirements and data sources, allowing for agile development.

3.   **Ethics and Privacy:** Ensure that pipelines adhere to ethical guidelines and protect sensitive data throughout the process.

Preparation Strategies:

1.   **Project Practice:** Work on end-to-end machine learning projects to gain hands-on experience in designing and implementing pipelines.

2.   **Tutorials and Courses:** Take online tutorials and courses on pipeline design, tools, and best practices.

3.   **Real-World Applications:** Explore open-source machine learning platforms (e.g., scikit-learn, TensorFlow, PyTorch) to understand pipeline implementation.

4.   **Peer Review:** Collaborate with peers or mentors to review and improve your pipeline design.

Designing and implementing machine learning pipelines is a critical skill that empowers data professionals to efficiently develop and deploy models, streamline workflows, and achieve consistent and reproducible results. Mastery of this skill enhances your ability to deliver effective solutions and contribute to the success of data-driven projects.

C. Demonstrating Critical Thinking and Problem Solving in Data Science and Big Data Analytics Interviews

Critical thinking and problem-solving skills are at the core of success in data science and big data analytics. These skills enable professionals to navigate complex challenges, analyze data effectively, and devise innovative solutions. In interviews, showcasing your ability to think critically and solve problems demonstrates your readiness to tackle real-world data-driven scenarios. Here's an in-depth exploration of how to effectively demonstrate critical thinking and problem-solving skills during interviews:

Analytical Approach:

1.   **Understanding the Problem:** Begin by thoroughly comprehending the problem statement or scenario. Identify the underlying question and the desired outcome.

2.   **Breaking Down Complexity:** Deconstruct complex problems into smaller, manageable components. This allows you to address each facet systematically.

3.   **Questioning Assumptions:** Challenge assumptions, and consider various angles to approach the problem. This demonstrates your ability to think beyond the obvious.

Data Exploration:

1.   **Curiosity and Inquisitiveness:** Be curious about the data. Explore distributions, relationships, and potential anomalies to uncover hidden insights.

2.   **Hypothesis Generation:** Formulate hypotheses based on your initial analysis. These hypotheses guide your exploration and problem-solving process.

Model Development:

1.   **Algorithm Selection:** Choose algorithms that align

with the problem and data characteristics. Explain your choices and how they address specific challenges.

2.   **Feature Engineering:** Tailor features to enhance model performance. Apply domain knowledge to extract meaningful information from data.

3.   **Parameter Tuning:** Experiment with different hyperparameters to optimize model performance. Explain your rationale for choosing specific values.

Iterative Refinement:

1.   **Continuous Improvement:** Approach problem-solving as an iterative process. Be open to refining your approach based on intermediate findings.

2.   **Learning from Failure:** Embrace failures or unsuccessful attempts as learning opportunities. Discuss how you adapted your strategy based on these experiences.

Communication:

1.   **Clarity in Explanation:** Articulate your thought process clearly. Narrate your steps, decisions, and insights as if you were teaching someone unfamiliar with the problem.

2.   **Visual Representation:** Utilize charts, graphs, and visualizations to convey your findings effectively. Visual aids

enhance understanding and engagement.

Domain Expertise:

1. **Contextual Understanding:** Relate the problem to its real-world context. Discuss how your insights could impact decision-making or business outcomes.

2. **Cross-Disciplinary Insights:** Draw insights from related domains, drawing connections that enrich your problem-solving approach.

Ethical Considerations:

1. **Ethical Lens:** Discuss how ethical considerations influence your approach, particularly when dealing with sensitive or potentially biased data.

2. **Transparency:** Be transparent about your assumptions, limitations, and potential biases in your analysis.

Preparation Strategies:

1. **Case Studies:** Work through case studies and datasets to practice your problem-solving skills and enhance your ability to derive insights.

2. **Mock Scenarios:** Engage in mock interviews or scenarios with peers or mentors to simulate interview conditions.

3. **Reading and Research:** Read about diverse problem-solving methodologies and apply them to various data scenarios.

4. **Reflective Practice:** Regularly reflect on your problem-solving approaches, noting areas for improvement and lessons learned.

5. **Stay Current:** Keep up with the latest advancements and methodologies in data science and big data analytics to expand your problem-solving toolkit.

By effectively demonstrating critical thinking and problem-solving skills in interviews, you showcase your ability to approach complex challenges with agility, creativity, and a structured approach. These skills not only position you as a capable candidate but also reflect your potential to contribute meaningfully to data-driven projects and initiatives.

CHAPTER 12

Behavioral Interview Preparation

Behavioral interviews in the realm of data science and big data analytics go beyond technical prowess, delving into your interpersonal skills, work ethic, and ability to navigate real-world scenarios. These interviews aim to assess your alignment with the organization's culture, your capacity to collaborate effectively, and your aptitude for ethical decision-making. Preparing for behavioral interviews involves reflecting on your past experiences, articulating your accomplishments, and showcasing qualities that make you a well-rounded and valuable member of a data-driven team. In this section, we delve into strategies and insights to excel in behavioral interviews and demonstrate your fit for the dynamic and collaborative world of data science.

A. Showcasing Soft Skills and Team Collaboration in Data Science and Big Data Analytics Interviews

In the fast-evolving landscape of data science and big data analytics, technical expertise alone is insufficient for success. Soft skills, including effective communication, teamwork, adaptability, and problem-solving, are equally essential. These skills enable professionals to collaborate harmoniously, drive innovation, and navigate the complexities of data-driven projects. During interviews, demonstrating your soft skills and ability to collaborate effectively within a team is key to showcasing your potential as a valuable asset. Here's an in-depth exploration of how to effectively showcase soft skills and team collaboration in interviews:

Effective Communication:

1.   **Clear Articulation:** Communicate your thoughts, ideas, and findings clearly and concisely. Avoid jargon and ensure your messages are understood by both technical and non-technical stakeholders.

2.   **Active Listening:** Listen attentively to others, seeking to understand their perspectives. This fosters productive discussions and demonstrates your respect for diverse viewpoints.

3.   **Questioning and Clarifying:** Ask thoughtful questions to gather more information and clarify any ambiguities. This showcases your engagement and commitment to understanding the task at hand.

Team Collaboration:

1.   **Interdisciplinary Collaboration:** Highlight instances where you've collaborated with individuals from diverse

backgrounds, contributing your data expertise to multidisciplinary teams.

2.   **Sharing Insights:** Explain how you've shared insights and findings in team settings, contributing valuable information that informed decisions or influenced project directions.

3.   **Constructive Feedback:** Discuss how you've provided constructive feedback to team members, helping them improve their work while maintaining a positive and supportive atmosphere.

4.   **Adaptability:** Describe situations where you've adapted your approach based on input from team members or evolving project requirements.

Problem-Solving and Adaptability:

1.   **Approach to Challenges:** Narrate how you've approached complex challenges by breaking them down into manageable steps, involving team members as needed.

2.   **Creative Solutions:** Showcase instances where you've proposed innovative solutions that deviated from conventional approaches, yielding positive outcomes.

3.   **Resilience:** Share experiences where you've encountered setbacks or unexpected obstacles and describe how you persevered, adapted, and ultimately succeeded.

Leadership and Followership:

1.   **Leading by Example:** Illustrate scenarios where you've taken the lead in guiding a team toward a shared goal, inspiring others with your work ethic and dedication.

2.   **Contributing as a Team Player:** Highlight situations where you've played a supportive role within a team, ensuring everyone's contributions were valued and acknowledged.

Ethical Decision-Making:

1.   **Ethical Considerations:** Discuss how you've approached ethical dilemmas in data collection, analysis, or interpretation. Emphasize your commitment to upholding integrity and transparency.

2.   **Balancing Priorities:** Share experiences where you've navigated situations involving conflicting interests, demonstrating your ability to weigh ethical concerns alongside project goals.

Preparation Strategies:

1.   **Reflect on Experiences:** Review your past experiences and identify instances that exemplify your soft skills and teamwork abilities.

2.   **Craft Stories:** Develop concise yet impactful stories that showcase how you've demonstrated soft skills and

collaborated within teams.

3. **Mock Interviews:** Conduct mock behavioral interviews with peers or mentors to practice articulating your soft skills in a structured manner.

4. **Feedback:** Seek feedback from trusted individuals to fine-tune your stories and responses, ensuring they effectively convey your strengths.

5. **Research the Company:** Understand the organization's values and culture to tailor your examples to align with their expectations.

6. **Learning and Growth:** Highlight instances where you've actively sought opportunities to learn from team members and enhance your collaborative skills.

Effectively showcasing soft skills and team collaboration in interviews underscores your ability to thrive in a collaborative and dynamic data-driven environment. These skills not only complement your technical prowess but also position you as a well-rounded candidate who can drive innovation, foster positive team dynamics, and contribute significantly to the success of data science and big data analytics projects.

B. Addressing Ethical and Privacy Concerns in Data Science and Big Data Analytics Interviews

The ethical and privacy implications of data science and big data analytics are becoming increasingly prominent in today's digital age. Professionals in these fields are entrusted with vast amounts of sensitive information, and their decisions can have far-reaching consequences. During interviews, demonstrating your understanding of ethical and privacy concerns, as well as your ability to navigate complex ethical dilemmas, is crucial to showcase your commitment to responsible data practices. Here's an in-depth exploration of how to effectively address ethical and privacy concerns in interviews:

Understanding Ethical and Privacy Concerns:

1.   **Data Privacy:** Discuss the importance of respecting individuals' privacy rights and securing personal data from unauthorized access or misuse.

2.   **Bias and Fairness:** Highlight the significance of mitigating bias in algorithms and ensuring fair treatment across different groups to avoid perpetuating discrimination.

3.   **Transparency:** Emphasize the need to provide clear explanations of data usage and modeling decisions to

stakeholders, enhancing transparency and trust.

4.　**Informed Consent:** Explain the concept of obtaining informed consent from individuals before collecting and using their data for analysis.

Navigating Ethical Dilemmas:

1.　**Scenario-Based Responses:** Be prepared to discuss hypothetical scenarios involving ethical challenges, such as handling biased data, addressing algorithmic bias, or preserving privacy.

2.　**Balancing Stakeholder Interests:** Demonstrate your ability to balance the interests of various stakeholders, considering ethical implications alongside business goals.

3.　**Decision-Making Process:** Walk through your decision-making process when facing an ethical dilemma. This could involve gathering information, consulting experts, and considering long-term consequences.

Data Handling and Anonymization:

1.　**Data Minimization:** Explain how you practice data minimization, collecting only the necessary data to achieve the intended analysis goals.

2.　**Anonymization Techniques:** Discuss methods you're

familiar with for anonymizing data to protect individuals' identities while preserving data utility.

Regulatory Compliance:

1.   **GDPR and Other Regulations:** Showcase your awareness of regulations such as the General Data Protection Regulation (GDPR) and how they impact data collection, storage, and usage.

2.   **Data Retention:** Discuss the importance of adhering to regulations regarding data retention and the responsible disposal of data.

Communication and Transparency:

1.   **Stakeholder Communication:** Describe how you communicate ethical considerations and privacy implications to both technical and non-technical stakeholders.

2.   **Ethical Documentation:** Explain how you document ethical decisions, privacy safeguards, and data usage protocols.

Preparation Strategies:

1.   **Research and Learning:** Familiarize yourself with ethical frameworks, privacy regulations, and best practices in data ethics.

2.   **Case Studies:** Review real-world case studies

involving ethical and privacy challenges to understand practical implications.

3.   **Current Events:** Stay informed about recent ethical controversies and privacy breaches to discuss them intelligently if relevant.

4.   **Discuss Ethical Projects:** If applicable, highlight projects where you've actively addressed ethical concerns and privacy considerations.

5.   **Sensitivity and Empathy:** Showcase your sensitivity to the potential impact of data decisions on individuals and society as a whole.

6.   **Interview Practice:** Engage in mock interviews to practice articulating your responses to ethical and privacy questions confidently.

Addressing ethical and privacy concerns demonstrates your commitment to responsible and thoughtful data practices. Your ability to navigate complex ethical dilemmas showcases your integrity, empathy, and holistic understanding of the multifaceted responsibilities of a data science and big data analytics professional.

C. Communicating Technical Concepts Clearly in Data Science and Big Data Analytics Interviews

Effective communication of technical concepts is an essential skill for data science and big data analytics professionals. The ability to convey complex ideas and insights in a clear and understandable manner is crucial for collaborating with both technical and non-technical stakeholders. During interviews, demonstrating your proficiency in explaining technical concepts can set you apart as a valuable team member who can bridge the gap between data expertise and practical application. Here's an in-depth exploration of how to communicate technical concepts clearly in interviews:

Understanding Your Audience:

1.   **Adaptability:** Tailor your communication style to suit your audience's level of technical understanding. Use simple language when speaking to non-technical stakeholders and more technical terms when discussing with fellow experts.

2.   **Stakeholder Needs:** Understand the specific needs and objectives of your audience. Adapt your explanations to address their concerns and expectations.

Clarity and Simplicity:

1.   **Succinct Explanations:** Present technical concepts

concisely, focusing on the key points that are relevant to the discussion or problem at hand.

2.   **Analogies and Metaphors:** Use relatable analogies and metaphors to connect technical ideas with familiar concepts, making it easier for your audience to grasp.

3.   **Step-by-Step Breakdown:** When explaining a complex process or algorithm, break it down into smaller, sequential steps. This provides a clear roadmap for understanding.

Visual Aids and Examples:

1.   **Visual Representations:** Utilize visual aids such as charts, diagrams, and graphs to illustrate technical concepts visually and enhance clarity.

2.   **Real-World Examples**: Anchor your explanations with real-world examples or case studies that highlight the practical implications of the technical concept.

Storytelling:

1.   **Narrative Structure:** Frame your explanation as a coherent story, leading your audience through the problem, solution, and impact of the technical concept.

2.   **Engaging Anecdotes:** Incorporate engaging anecdotes or scenarios that capture your audience's interest and

demonstrate the real-world relevance of the concept.

Interactive Engagement:

1.   **Question and Answer:** Encourage questions from your audience and address them patiently. This fosters engagement and clarifies any points of confusion.

2.   **Hands-On Demonstration:** If feasible, offer a hands-on demonstration or interactive walkthrough to provide a tangible understanding of the concept.

Practice Active Listening:

1.   **Feedback Loop:** Pay attention to your audience's reactions and body language. Adjust your explanation based on their cues to ensure comprehension.

2.   **Checking for Understanding:** Periodically pause during your explanation to check if your audience is following along. Encourage them to ask for clarifications.

Preparation Strategies:

1.   **Practice Elevator Pitch:** Prepare concise elevator pitches for technical concepts, explaining them in under a minute.

2.   **Teaching Experience:** Draw from any experience you have in teaching or mentoring to showcase your ability to convey complex ideas effectively.

3.   **Peer Review:** Seek feedback from peers or mentors on your explanations to identify areas for improvement.

4.   **Communication Workshops:** Participate in communication workshops or courses to enhance your verbal and visual communication skills.

5.   **Documenting and Rehearsing:** Create scripts or outlines for explaining common technical concepts. Practice delivering these explanations until they become natural.

Effective communication of technical concepts is a valuable skill that not only helps you excel in interviews but also enhances your ability to collaborate, lead, and contribute effectively in data science and big data analytics projects. Clear communication bridges the gap between technical expertise and real-world application, making you an invaluable asset to your team and organization.

Part V

Conducting Data Science and Big Data Analytics Interviews

CHAPTER 13

The Interviewer's Role in Data Science and Big Data Analytics Interviews

The role of an interviewer in data science and big data analytics interviews is pivotal in assessing candidates' skills, experiences, and suitability for roles in this dynamic and rapidly evolving field. Interviewers play a multifaceted role, encompassing responsibilities that range from evaluating technical expertise and problem-solving abilities to assessing soft skills, ethical considerations, and potential contributions to the organization. In this section, we explore the various dimensions of the interviewer's role and how their expertise shapes the interview process, ultimately identifying candidates who can thrive in the challenging and impactful world of data science and big data analytics.

A. Designing Relevant and Effective Interview Questions in Data Science and Big Data Analytics

Crafting well-structured and insightful interview questions is a critical aspect of the interviewer's role in data science and big data analytics. Thoughtfully designed questions not only assess a candidate's technical proficiency but also reveal their problem-solving strategies, critical thinking abilities, and alignment with the organization's values. In this in-depth exploration, we delve into the art of designing relevant and effective interview questions that rigorously evaluate candidates and contribute to selecting the best-fit talent:

Understanding the Interview Goals:

1. **Skill Assessment:** Define the specific skills, competencies, and knowledge areas you aim to evaluate in the interview.

2. **Cultural Fit:** Craft questions that probe a candidate's compatibility with the company culture, ethics, and collaborative dynamics.

3. **Problem-Solving:** Design questions that simulate real-world challenges to assess the candidate's analytical thinking and approach to complex issues.

Types of Interview Questions:

1. **Technical Proficiency:** Pose questions that gauge a candidate's understanding of programming languages, statistical methods, machine learning algorithms, and big data tools.

2. **Case Studies:** Present scenarios or datasets that reflect the challenges the organization faces. Evaluate how candidates approach and solve these problems.

3.   **Behavioral Questions:** Inquire about past experiences and accomplishments to assess how candidates handle teamwork, conflicts, and ethical dilemmas.

Question Design Best Practices:

1.   **Specificity:** Craft questions that are precise and focused on a particular skill or concept. Ambiguity can lead to vague responses.

2.   **Open-Ended:** Frame questions in a way that encourages candidates to provide detailed responses, showcasing their depth of knowledge and problem-solving process.

3.   **Real-World Relevance:** Ensure questions reflect the challenges and tasks candidates will encounter in the role. This aligns the assessment with the actual job requirements.

4.   **Progressive Complexity:** Gradually increase the complexity of questions to assess a candidate's knowledge depth and adaptability to different scenarios.

Assessing Technical Proficiency:

1.   **Coding and Algorithmic Challenges:** Pose coding exercises or algorithmic problems to evaluate a candidate's coding skills, algorithm design, and optimization abilities.

2.   **Model Implementation:** Request candidates to

implement machine learning models, assess their understanding of model selection, feature engineering, and evaluation metrics.

Problem-Solving and Critical Thinking:

1.   **Scenario-Based Challenges:** Present candidates with data-driven scenarios that mirror real-world challenges. Evaluate their approach, assumptions, and decision-making.

2.   **Creative Thinking:** Include questions that require candidates to think outside the box, proposing innovative solutions beyond conventional methods.

Behavioral and Soft Skills:

1.   **Collaboration and Communication:** Craft questions that assess a candidate's ability to communicate complex technical concepts to both technical and non-technical stakeholders.

2.   **Ethical Considerations:** Pose scenarios involving ethical dilemmas to evaluate a candidate's awareness of data ethics and their ability to navigate morally complex situations.

Feedback and Iteration:

1.   **Continuous Improvement:** Solicit feedback from interviewers, candidates, and stakeholders to refine and optimize your interview questions over time.

2.   **Pilot Testing:** Test new interview questions with

current team members to ensure they effectively capture the desired skills and competencies.

Preparation Strategies:

1.   **Question Banks:** Develop a repository of interview questions that cover a wide range of technical and soft skills.

2.   **Interview Training:** Provide interviewers with training on how to ask questions effectively, evaluate responses, and provide constructive feedback.

3.   **Regular Review:** Periodically review and update your question bank to reflect emerging trends, technologies, and challenges in the data science field.

Designing relevant and effective interview questions requires a deep understanding of the competencies and attributes required for success in data science and big data analytics roles. Thoughtful question design enables interviewers to assess candidates comprehensively, uncovering their technical prowess, problem-solving acumen, and alignment with the organization's values and goals.

B.   Assessing Data Science and Big Data Analytics Expertise in Interviews

Evaluating a candidate's expertise in data science and big data analytics is a multifaceted process that requires a comprehensive understanding of the field's technical intricacies, problem-solving abilities, and practical application. Interviewers play a crucial role in assessing a candidate's depth of knowledge, critical thinking skills, and proficiency in leveraging data to drive insights and value. In this in-depth exploration, we delve into the methods, considerations, and strategies for effectively assessing data science and big data analytics expertise during interviews:

Technical Proficiency:

1.   **Algorithmic Understanding:** Pose questions that assess a candidate's familiarity with fundamental algorithms, statistical techniques, and machine learning models.

2.   **Data Manipulation:** Evaluate a candidate's skills in data cleaning, transformation, and feature engineering. Pose scenarios involving messy datasets to gauge their ability to handle real-world data challenges.

3.   **Programming   Proficiency:**   Present   coding challenges to assess a candidate's programming skills, code efficiency, and understanding of libraries and frameworks like Python, R, or TensorFlow.

Modeling and Analysis:

1.   **Model Selection:** Inquire about the candidate's process for selecting appropriate models based on problem

characteristics, dataset size, and goals.

2. **Feature Engineering:** Evaluate a candidate's ability to engineer relevant features from raw data, enhancing the predictive power of machine learning models.

3. **Evaluation Metrics:** Pose questions about different evaluation metrics (e.g., accuracy, precision, recall, F1-score) and their relevance for specific problem domains.

Big Data Technologies:

1. **Data Storage and Processing:** Assess familiarity with big data storage solutions (e.g., HDFS, S3) and processing frameworks (e.g., MapReduce, Apache Spark).

2. **Distributed Computing:** Inquire about a candidate's experience in leveraging parallel and distributed computing to handle large-scale data processing.

Practical Problem-Solving:

1. **Case Studies:** Present candidates with real-world case studies or datasets that reflect challenges commonly encountered in data science and big data analytics projects.

2. **Scenario-Based Questions:** Pose hypothetical scenarios involving complex data challenges and evaluate how candidates approach problem-solving step by step.

Interdisciplinary Knowledge:

1.   **Business Understanding:** Assess a candidate's ability to relate technical insights to business goals, demonstrating their strategic thinking and alignment with organizational objectives.

2.   **Ethical Considerations:** Inquire about candidates' awareness of ethical dilemmas in data analysis and their approach to handling sensitive or biased data.

Communication and Visualization:

1.   **Explaining Technical Concepts:** Evaluate a candidate's ability to articulate complex technical concepts clearly and concisely to both technical and non-technical stakeholders.

2.   **Data Visualization:** Request candidates to interpret and visualize data effectively, demonstrating their skill in conveying insights through compelling visual representations.

Learning and Adaptability:

1.   **Continuous Learning:** Discuss the candidate's approach to staying current with evolving data science techniques, tools, and best practices.

2.   **Adaptability:** Inquire about instances where the candidate adapted their skills and approach to address novel or unexpected data challenges.

Preparation Strategies:

1. **Standardized Evaluation Criteria:** Develop a clear rubric or set of evaluation criteria to ensure consistency in assessing candidates across interviewers.

2. **Question Calibration:** Calibrate interview questions with the team to ensure they accurately reflect the skills and competencies desired for the role.

3. **Scoring and Documentation:** Develop a scoring system to objectively evaluate each candidate's performance. Document detailed feedback to support the decision-making process.

4. **Interviewer Training:** Train interviewers on effective assessment methods, questioning techniques, and providing constructive feedback.

5. **Peer Review:** Engage in peer review sessions to collectively evaluate candidate responses, fostering diverse perspectives and insights.

6. **Industry Best Practices:** Stay informed about the latest trends, methodologies, and challenges in data science and big data analytics to ensure your assessment criteria remain current and relevant.

Assessing data science and big data analytics expertise in

interviews is a dynamic and iterative process that requires a deep understanding of the field's nuances. Thoughtful evaluation methods, well-designed questions, and comprehensive assessment strategies empower interviewers to identify candidates who possess the technical acumen, analytical thinking, and problem-solving skills necessary to excel in the ever-evolving landscape of data-driven decision-making.

C. Evaluating Communication and Analytical Abilities in Data Science and Big Data Analytics Interviews

Assessing a candidate's communication and analytical abilities is paramount in data science and big data analytics interviews. Effective communication ensures that insights are conveyed clearly to stakeholders, while strong analytical skills are crucial for drawing meaningful conclusions from complex datasets. Interviewers play a pivotal role in evaluating these competencies, as they provide insights into a candidate's capacity to translate technical findings into actionable insights and collaborate within interdisciplinary teams. In this in-depth exploration, we delve into methods, considerations, and strategies for rigorously evaluating communication and analytical abilities during interviews:

Communication Abilities:

1. **Clarity of Explanation:** Evaluate how well

candidates articulate complex technical concepts in a clear and concise manner. Are they able to break down intricate ideas into understandable explanations?

2.   **Adaptability:** Assess a candidate's ability to tailor their communication style to different audiences, spanning technical experts and non-technical stakeholders.

3.   **Storytelling:** Evaluate their storytelling skills by assessing their capability to frame technical insights within a coherent narrative, making data-driven findings relatable and impactful.

4.   **Visual Communication:** Inquire about their use of data visualization techniques to enhance their communication of insights. How effectively do they convey complex information through visuals?

Analytical Abilities:

1.   **Problem-Solving Approach:** Pose hypothetical analytical challenges and assess the candidate's step-by-step problem-solving strategy, including hypothesis generation, data exploration, and model selection.

2.   **Critical Thinking:** Evaluate their capacity to question assumptions, identify potential biases, and consider multiple angles when analyzing data and drawing conclusions.

3.   **Data Interpretation:** Present candidates with datasets or graphs and gauge their ability to interpret trends, anomalies, and patterns within the data.

4.   **Handling Ambiguity:** Assess how candidates handle situations where data is incomplete, noisy, or ambiguous. Do they demonstrate adaptability and an effective approach to handling uncertainties?

Collaboration and Teamwork:

1.   **Interdisciplinary Engagement:** Discuss experiences where candidates collaborated with individuals from diverse backgrounds, highlighting their ability to work seamlessly within multidisciplinary teams.

2.   **Contributions to Decision-Making:** Inquire about their role in influencing decisions through data-driven insights, showcasing their value as analytical contributors.

3.   **Conflict Resolution:** Pose scenarios involving conflicting viewpoints within a team and assess their ability to navigate disagreements while maintaining a positive collaborative environment.

Ethical Considerations:

1.   **Ethical Communication:** Evaluate how candidates address ethical considerations in their communication, including

data privacy, bias mitigation, and transparency in presenting findings.

2.   **Balancing Accuracy and Interpretability:** Assess their approach to communicating nuanced insights while avoiding oversimplification or misrepresentation of data.

Preparation Strategies:

1.   **Behavioral Interviews:** Include scenario-based questions that require candidates to explain their analytical and communication strategies in previous projects or work experiences.

2.   **Interactive Problem-Solving:** Incorporate collaborative exercises or real-time data interpretation tasks to assess how candidates engage in analytical discussions.

3.   **Presentation Assessment:** Request candidates to deliver short presentations on a technical topic, evaluating their ability to structure content, engage the audience, and convey insights effectively.

4.   **Mock Scenarios:** Engage in mock interviews with peers or mentors to practice articulating insights clearly and responding to analytical challenges on the spot.

5.   **Feedback Loop:** Continuously refine your assessment methods based on feedback from candidates, team members, and

fellow interviewers.

6.   **Benchmarking:** Establish benchmarks or scoring criteria for evaluating communication and analytical abilities, promoting consistency across interviews.

Evaluating communication and analytical abilities goes beyond technical prowess, illuminating a candidate's capacity to collaborate, influence decision-making, and effectively drive data-driven insights. By applying thoughtful assessment methods and aligning them with the role's demands, interviewers contribute to identifying candidates who possess the holistic skill set required to thrive in the data-driven world of data science and big data analytics.

CHAPTER 14

Interview Process Management in Data Science and Big Data Analytics

The interview process management for data science and big data analytics roles is a strategic and structured approach to selecting the best-suited candidates who can contribute to a data-driven organization's success. Effective interview process management involves orchestrating various stages of assessment, coordinating with stakeholders, and ensuring a fair and rigorous evaluation process. In this section, we explore the essential components of interview process management, from structuring interview rounds to collaborating with hiring managers and HR, to ultimately identify individuals who possess the skills, expertise, and qualities required for excellence in the realm of data science and big data analytics.

A. Structuring Technical and Behavioral Interview Rounds in Data Science and Big Data Analytics

The process of hiring for data science and big data analytics roles involves carefully designed interview rounds that assess both technical prowess and soft skills. Structuring these rounds effectively is crucial to comprehensively evaluate candidates and select individuals who can excel in this complex and dynamic field. In this in-depth exploration, we delve into the considerations, strategies, and best practices for structuring technical and behavioral interview rounds:

Technical Interview Rounds:

1.   **Skills Assessment:** Define the technical competencies required for the role, such as programming, statistical analysis, machine learning, and big data technologies.

2.   **Coding and Algorithmic Challenges:** Present coding exercises that mirror tasks candidates might encounter in real projects. Evaluate their coding proficiency, algorithm design, and problem-solving skills.

3.   **Model Implementation and Analysis:** Request candidates to build and interpret machine learning models. Assess their ability to select appropriate algorithms, handle data preprocessing, and evaluate model performance.

4.   **Big Data Technologies:** Pose questions or scenarios that assess candidates' familiarity with big data storage, processing frameworks, and distributed computing concepts.

5.   **Case Studies:** Design scenarios based on real-world challenges in data science and big data analytics. Evaluate

candidates' ability to analyze data, propose solutions, and communicate findings effectively.

Behavioral Interview Rounds:

1.   **Scenario-Based Questions:** Pose hypothetical scenarios that require candidates to demonstrate their problem-solving approach, collaboration skills, and ethical considerations.

2.   **Communication and Collaboration:** Assess how candidates communicate complex technical concepts to both technical and non-technical stakeholders. Inquire about their experiences working within cross-functional teams.

3.   **Conflict Resolution and Adaptability:** Evaluate candidates' ability to handle disagreements within a team and their approach to adapting to evolving project requirements.

4.   **Leadership and Ethical Dilemmas:** Present situations involving leadership responsibilities or ethical challenges. Assess candidates' decision-making, empathy, and ethical considerations.

Integration of Rounds:

1.   **Balanced Evaluation:** Ensure a balance between technical and behavioral rounds to comprehensively assess a candidate's skills, problem-solving abilities, and alignment with company values.

2.   **Sequential or Parallel:** Decide whether technical and behavioral rounds will be conducted sequentially or concurrently, considering logistical constraints and candidate experience.

Candidate Experience:

1.   **Clarity and Expectations:** Clearly communicate the structure and expectations of each interview round to candidates, fostering transparency and reducing anxiety.

2.   **Engagement:** Create an engaging and interactive environment that allows candidates to showcase their skills, discuss their experiences, and interact with interviewers.

Assessment Criteria:

1.   **Standardized Rubrics:** Develop standardized rubrics or scoring guidelines to ensure consistent evaluation across interviewers and candidates.

2.   **Objective Evaluation:** Use objective assessment methods, such as scoring coding exercises or evaluating specific criteria, to minimize bias and ensure fair evaluation.

Feedback and Iteration:

1.   **Post-Interview Discussions:** Facilitate discussions among interviewers to share insights, align on evaluations, and collectively determine a candidate's fit.

2. **Continuous Improvement:** Regularly review and refine the structure of technical and behavioral rounds based on feedback from interviewers and candidates.

Preparation Strategies:

1. **Round-Specific Training:** Provide interviewers with specialized training for technical and behavioral rounds, focusing on relevant evaluation criteria and best practices.

2. **Mock Interviews:** Engage in mock interview sessions with peers or mentors to practice effectively structuring and conducting technical and behavioral rounds.

3. **Candidate Feedback:** Solicit feedback from candidates about their interview experience, including the clarity of round expectations and the assessment process.

Structuring technical and behavioral interview rounds requires a thoughtful approach that captures both the technical depth and interpersonal skills needed for success in data science and big data analytics roles. By aligning these rounds with the role's demands and company culture, interviewers contribute to a rigorous evaluation process that identifies candidates who possess the holistic skill set necessary to excel in the dynamic and impactful world of data-driven decision-making.

B. Collaborating with Hiring Managers and HR in Data Science and Big Data Analytics Interviews

Effective collaboration between interviewers, hiring managers, and HR professionals is essential for successfully identifying and selecting the right candidates for data science and big data analytics roles. This collaborative effort ensures that the interview process is aligned with the organization's goals, culture, and job requirements. In this in-depth exploration, we delve into the considerations, strategies, and best practices for collaborating with hiring managers and HR throughout the interview process:

Defining Role Requirements:

1.   **Initial Alignment:** Collaborate with hiring managers to establish a clear understanding of the specific skills, qualifications, and competencies required for the data science or big data analytics role.

2.   **Role Clarity:** Work closely with HR to develop accurate and detailed job descriptions that reflect the role's responsibilities, technical requirements, and desired soft skills.

Interview Process Design:

1.   **Technical Assessment:** Collaborate with hiring managers to design technical interview rounds that accurately assess candidates' abilities to perform the tasks and solve the

problems relevant to the role.

2.   **Behavioral Evaluation:** Work with HR to develop behavioral interview questions that align with the organization's values, culture, and expectations for teamwork, communication, and ethical considerations.

3.   **Timeline and Logistics:** Collaboratively establish a clear interview schedule, communication plan, and logistics to ensure a smooth and well-coordinated interview process.

Candidate Evaluation and Feedback:

1.   **Assessment Criteria:** Collaborate with hiring managers to develop a standardized rubric or scoring system for evaluating candidates' technical, analytical, and soft skills.

2.   **Feedback Loop:** Work closely with HR to collect feedback from interviewers, consolidate evaluations, and facilitate post-interview discussions to ensure a well-rounded assessment.

Candidate Experience:

1.   **Communication:** Collaborate with HR to ensure transparent and timely communication with candidates throughout the interview process, managing expectations and providing updates.

2.   **Engagement:** Collaboratively design an engaging and

positive candidate experience that reflects the organization's values and commitment to professionalism.

Diversity and Inclusion:

1. **Bias Mitigation:** Work with HR to implement strategies for minimizing unconscious bias in the interview process, fostering a fair and inclusive evaluation.

2. **Diverse Panel:** Collaborate on assembling diverse interview panels that represent different perspectives, enhancing the validity and fairness of evaluations.

Evaluation Consistency:

1. **Calibration:** Collaborate with HR to conduct calibration sessions to align interviewers' understanding of evaluation criteria, ensuring consistency and fairness.

2. **Data-Driven Insights:** Utilize HR analytics and data to track and analyze interview outcomes, identifying trends and areas for improvement.

Feedback and Continuous Improvement:

1. **Post-Interview Review:** Collaborate with hiring managers and HR to review the interview process, gather feedback from interviewers, and identify opportunities for enhancement.

2. **Iterative Refinement:** Continuously refine the

interview process based on feedback, candidate experience, and evolving organizational needs.

Preparation Strategies:

1.   **Regular Meetings:** Schedule regular meetings with hiring managers and HR to discuss candidate pipelines, assessment strategies, and process improvements.

2.   **Cross-Functional Training:** Facilitate cross-functional training sessions where interviewers, hiring managers, and HR professionals share insights and best practices.

3.   **Candidate Journey Mapping:** Collaborate with HR to map out the candidate journey, identifying touchpoints where collaboration can enhance the overall experience.

Collaborating effectively with hiring managers and HR ensures a seamless and well-structured interview process that identifies top talent aligned with the organization's values, requirements, and culture. By leveraging each other's expertise and perspectives, interviewers, hiring managers, and HR professionals contribute to a comprehensive assessment that accurately evaluates candidates' skills, experience, and potential to excel in data science and big data analytics roles.

C. Providing Constructive Feedback and Evaluation in Data Science and Big Data Analytics Interviews

The process of providing constructive feedback and evaluation to candidates is a crucial aspect of the interview process for data science and big data analytics roles. Thoughtful and actionable feedback not only helps candidates understand their strengths and areas for improvement but also contributes to the overall refinement of the interview process. In this in-depth exploration, we delve into the considerations, strategies, and best practices for providing constructive feedback and evaluation:

Importance of Constructive Feedback:

1. **Professional Development:** Constructive feedback provides candidates with insights into their performance, enabling them to identify growth areas and enhance their skills.

2. **Candidate Experience:** Timely and thoughtful feedback enhances the candidate experience, reflecting the organization's commitment to transparency and professionalism.

Timeliness and Clarity:

1. **Promptness:** Provide feedback as soon as possible after the interview to ensure that the candidate's performance is fresh in their mind.

2.   **Specificity:** Offer specific examples of the candidate's strengths and areas for improvement, using detailed observations to support your feedback.

3.   **Balanced Feedback**: Acknowledge both strengths and areas needing improvement, ensuring a well-rounded assessment.

Actionable Feedback:

1.   **Concrete Suggestions:** Provide actionable recommendations for how candidates can enhance their skills or address identified weaknesses.

2.   **Skill-Based:** Tailor feedback to the specific skills and competencies relevant to the role, focusing on technical, analytical, and soft skills.

Behavioral Feedback:

1.   **Scenario-Based:** Use scenarios or examples from the interview to illustrate behavioral feedback, demonstrating how candidates responded to specific challenges.

2.   **Impact on Teamwork:** Highlight instances where candidates displayed effective collaboration, communication, and ethical considerations.

Technical Feedback:

1.   **Coding and Problem-Solving:** Evaluate code quality,

efficiency, and problem-solving strategies, providing guidance on improving coding practices.

2.   **Model Interpretation:** Offer insights into candidates' understanding of machine learning models, feature engineering, and interpretation of results.

Communication Feedback:

1.   **Clarity and Storytelling:** Assess candidates' ability to explain technical concepts clearly and coherently. Offer suggestions for improving narrative and storytelling.

2.   **Visual Communication:** Comment on candidates' data visualization techniques and how effectively they conveyed insights through visuals.

Delivering Feedback:

1.   **Constructive Tone:** Provide feedback in a positive and supportive manner, focusing on growth opportunities rather than criticism.

2.   **Open Dialogue:** Encourage candidates to ask questions, seek clarification, and engage in a dialogue about the feedback provided.

Candidate Engagement:

1.   **Feedback Discussion:** Offer candidates the

opportunity to discuss the feedback, addressing any questions or concerns they may have.

2. **Learning Opportunities:** Highlight the potential for continued skill development and suggest resources for self-improvement.

Continuous Improvement:

1. **Feedback Loop:** Share insights and feedback with hiring managers and HR to collectively assess candidate performance and refine the interview process.

2. **Reviewer Calibration:** Engage in calibration sessions with fellow interviewers to ensure consistency and alignment in feedback and evaluation.

Preparation Strategies:

1. **Feedback Training:** Provide interviewers with training on effective feedback delivery, emphasizing the importance of clarity, objectivity, and professionalism.

2. **Peer Review:** Engage in peer review sessions to practice providing feedback and receive input on your own feedback delivery.

3. **Documentation:** Document feedback in a structured and organized manner, ensuring that it can be easily referenced

and shared with stakeholders.

Providing constructive feedback and evaluation requires a delicate balance of offering insightful guidance and maintaining a positive and respectful tone. By focusing on actionable recommendations, engaging in open dialogue, and collaborating with hiring managers and HR, interviewers contribute to candidates' professional growth and development while continuously improving the interview process for data science and big data analytics roles.

CHAPTER 15

Ethical and Professional Interview Practices in Data Science and Big Data Analytics

Ethical and professional interview practices are integral to the recruitment process for data science and big data analytics roles. Adhering to high ethical standards and maintaining a professional demeanor ensures fairness, respect, and transparency throughout the evaluation process. In this section, we explore the fundamental principles, considerations, and best practices that guide ethical and professional conduct during interviews, safeguarding both candidates and organizations in the data-driven realm.

A. Ensuring Fairness and Equal Opportunity in Data Science and Big Data Analytics Interviews

In the context of data science and big data analytics interviews, ensuring fairness and equal opportunity is not only a moral imperative but also a critical step toward building diverse and inclusive teams that drive innovation and excellence. Fair and unbiased interview practices contribute to a level playing field where candidates from all backgrounds can showcase their skills and potential. In this comprehensive exploration, we delve into the principles, strategies, and best practices for fostering fairness and equal opportunity throughout the interview process:

Principles of Fairness and Equal Opportunity:

1.   **Non-Discrimination:** Treat all candidates consistently, regardless of factors such as race, gender, age, ethnicity, disability, or socioeconomic background.

2.   **Merit-Based Evaluation:** Base decisions solely on candidates' qualifications, skills, and competencies relevant to the role.

3.   **Minimization of Bias:** Implement strategies to minimize unconscious biases that can influence decision-making, promoting an objective and impartial evaluation.

Job Posting and Recruitment:

1.   **Inclusive Language:** Craft job descriptions and postings that use inclusive language, appealing to a diverse pool of candidates.

2.   **Diverse Outreach:** Proactively seek out diverse candidate pipelines through various channels, including underrepresented groups and professional networks.

Interview Panel Diversity:

1.   **Representation:** Ensure that interview panels comprise individuals from diverse backgrounds and perspectives to mitigate bias and enhance evaluation accuracy.

2.   **Bias Awareness Training:** Provide interviewers with training on recognizing and mitigating biases to promote consistent and unbiased assessments.

Interview Content and Format:

1.   **Role-Relevant Criteria:** Develop interview questions and evaluations that focus on skills and competencies directly related to the job requirements.

2.   **Structured Interviews**: Use standardized interview formats and evaluation criteria to ensure uniform assessment and comparison of candidates.

Candidate Experience:

1.   **Accessibility:** Accommodate candidates' individual needs, such as physical accessibility or remote interview options, to ensure equal participation.

2.   **Transparent Communication:** Provide clear information about the interview process, expectations, and evaluation criteria to create a level playing field for all candidates.

Bias Mitigation Strategies:

1.   **Blind Review:** Implement blind review practices where relevant, such as anonymizing resumes or coding submissions, to reduce unconscious bias.

2.   **Diverse Scenarios:** Pose scenarios and questions that reflect a variety of experiences and backgrounds, avoiding assumptions or stereotypes.

Assessment Consistency:

1.   **Calibration Sessions:** Conduct calibration sessions among interviewers to align on evaluation criteria and ensure uniform assessment standards.

2.   **Structured Evaluation:** Develop rubrics or scoring guidelines that focus on specific skills and competencies, minimizing subjective interpretations.

Data-Driven Insights:

1.   **Analysis and Monitoring:** Regularly analyze interview outcomes to identify any patterns of bias or disparities in evaluation results.

2.   **Adjustments and Iteration:** Use data insights to make informed adjustments to the interview process, continuously striving for fairness and equal opportunity.

Preparation Strategies:

1.   **Training and Awareness:** Educate interviewers, hiring managers, and HR professionals about the importance of fairness, equal opportunity, and bias mitigation.

2.   **Diversity Advocacy:** Foster a culture of diversity and inclusion within the organization, where all team members advocate for fair practices.

Ensuring fairness and equal opportunity in data science and big data analytics interviews goes beyond compliance; it is a commitment to creating an inclusive environment that values diversity and promotes innovation. By adhering to these principles and strategies, interviewers contribute to an ethical and professional interview process that empowers candidates to showcase their skills, regardless of their background, and enables organizations to build stronger, more dynamic teams.

B.   Respecting Candidate Privacy and Data in Data Science and Big Data Analytics Interviews

In the era of data-driven decision-making, respecting candidate privacy and data is a paramount ethical responsibility during the interview process for data science and big data analytics roles. As custodians of sensitive information, interviewers and organizations must uphold rigorous standards to safeguard candidate privacy, maintain data security, and ensure compliance with relevant regulations. In this comprehensive exploration, we delve into the principles, considerations, and best practices for respecting candidate privacy and data throughout the interview process:

Principles of Candidate Privacy and Data Respect:

1. **Informed Consent:** Obtain explicit and informed consent from candidates regarding the collection, storage, and usage of their personal and assessment data.

2. **Transparency:** Communicate openly with candidates about how their data will be used, who will have access to it, and how long it will be retained.

3. **Minimization:** Collect only the data necessary for the interview process, minimizing the scope of information gathered.

Data Collection and Usage:

1. **Purpose Limitation:** Clearly articulate the purpose for collecting candidate data and ensure that it is used exclusively for interview-related assessment and evaluation.

2. **Data Security:** Implement robust security measures to protect candidate data from unauthorized access, breaches, or misuse.

3. **Anonymization:** Anonymize candidate data whenever

possible, especially during the assessment of technical skills, to minimize potential bias.

Third-Party Tools and Platforms:

1.   **Vendor Compliance:** If utilizing third-party tools or platforms for interviews, ensure that they adhere to data protection standards and comply with relevant regulations.

2.   **Data Sharing:** Limit the sharing of candidate data with third parties to only those involved in the interview and evaluation process.

Data Retention and Deletion:

1.   **Retention Period:** Clearly define the duration for which candidate data will be retained and ensure compliance with data retention laws.

2.   **Deletion Protocol**: Establish protocols for securely deleting candidate data after the specified retention period expires.

Candidate Consent and Rights:

1.   **Access and Correction:** Provide candidates with the right to access their personal data, request corrections, and inquire about the status of their information.

2.   **Withdrawal of Consent:** Inform candidates of their right to withdraw consent for data collection and usage, and ensure

that the process for doing so is straightforward.

Communication and Transparency:

1.   **Privacy Policy:** Develop a transparent privacy policy that outlines the organization's practices regarding candidate data collection, usage, retention, and security.

2.   **Candidate Communication:** Clearly explain the organization's data protection practices to candidates, addressing any concerns they may have.

Legal and Regulatory Compliance:

1.   **Data Protection Laws:** Familiarize yourself with relevant data protection regulations, such as GDPR, CCPA, or local laws, and ensure compliance in all aspects of the interview process.

2.   **Cross-Border Data Transfer:** If applicable, ensure that candidate data is transferred across borders in compliance with data protection laws.

Preparation Strategies:

1.   **Privacy Training:** Provide interviewers and relevant staff with training on data protection, privacy, and legal requirements.

2.   **Data Protection Officer:** Appoint a data protection

officer or designate a responsible individual to oversee candidate data protection.

Respecting candidate privacy and data integrity is an ethical imperative that reinforces an organization's commitment to professionalism, trustworthiness, and responsible data management. By upholding these principles and best practices, interviewers and organizations create a secure and transparent environment that fosters confidence among candidates and demonstrates their dedication to ethical conduct in the data science and big data analytics interview process.

C. Upholding Ethical and Professional Standards in Data Science and Big Data Analytics Interviews

Upholding ethical and professional standards in the interview process for data science and big data analytics roles is not only a reflection of an organization's values but also a foundational pillar that fosters trust, integrity, and credibility. Adhering to rigorous ethical guidelines ensures that candidates are treated with respect, fairness, and transparency, while maintaining the high standards expected in the data-driven industry. In this comprehensive exploration, we delve into the principles, considerations, and best practices for upholding ethical and professional standards throughout the interview process:

Ethical Principles in Interviews:

1.   **Integrity:** Conduct interviews with honesty, transparency, and consistency, adhering to ethical norms in interactions and evaluations.

2.   **Confidentiality:** Safeguard candidate information and discussions, respecting confidentiality and not disclosing sensitive details without explicit consent.

3.   **Fairness:** Treat all candidates impartially, ensuring that every individual has an equal opportunity to showcase their skills and potential.

Professional Conduct:

1.   **Respectful Engagement:** Maintain a respectful and courteous demeanor during interviews, creating an environment where candidates feel valued and at ease.

2.   **Objective Evaluation:** Evaluate candidates objectively, focusing solely on their qualifications, skills, and fit for the role.

Interview Process Considerations:

1.   **Inclusive Environment:** Foster an inclusive and welcoming interview environment that accommodates candidates' diverse backgrounds, needs, and circumstances.

2.   **Timely Communication:** Provide candidates with clear and timely communication about the interview process, expectations, and outcomes.

Candidate Feedback and Communication:

1.   **Constructive Feedback:** Offer feedback that is actionable, respectful, and focused on helping candidates improve their skills and performance.

2.   **Transparency:** Clearly explain the evaluation criteria and rationale behind assessment decisions, promoting transparency and trust.

Handling Ethical Dilemmas:

1.   **Scenario-Based Questions:** Pose ethical scenarios that require candidates to navigate complex decisions, demonstrating their ability to approach challenges with integrity.

2.   **Discussion of Values:** Engage in discussions about ethical considerations in data science, including privacy, bias mitigation, and responsible data use.

Mitigating Bias and Discrimination:

1.   **Unconscious Bias Awareness:** Be mindful of unconscious biases that may influence perceptions and decisions, employing strategies to mitigate their impact.

2.   **Diversity and Inclusion:** Ensure that interview practices and questions do not discriminate based on gender, race, age, or other protected characteristics.

Data Privacy and Consent:

1.   **Candidate Consent:** Obtain informed consent from candidates regarding the collection, usage, and retention of their personal and assessment data.

2.   **Data Handling:** Handle candidate data in compliance with relevant data protection laws and organizational policies.

Preparation Strategies:

1.   **Ethics Training:** Provide interviewers with training on ethical considerations in data science and big data analytics, emphasizing respect, fairness, and integrity.

2.   **Scenario Workshops:** Conduct workshops where interviewers collaboratively discuss ethical scenarios, promoting awareness and alignment on ethical standards.

3.   **Code of Conduct:** Develop and share a comprehensive code of conduct for interviewers, outlining the organization's expectations for ethical behavior.

4.   **Peer Review:** Engage in peer review sessions to reflect on ethical considerations and gather input on interview techniques

and questions.

Upholding ethical and professional standards in data science and big data analytics interviews is not only a reflection of an organization's commitment to responsible conduct but also an investment in building a positive reputation, fostering candidate trust, and contributing to the advancement of the field. By embracing these principles and best practices, interviewers contribute to a fair, respectful, and transparent interview process that aligns with the highest ethical and professional standards.

Conclusion

As we draw the final curtain on this journey through these pages, we invite you to reflect on the knowledge, insights, and discoveries that have unfolded before you. Our exploration of various subjects has been a captivating voyage into the depths of understanding.

In these chapters, we have ventured through the intricacies of numerous topics and examined the key concepts and findings that define these fields. It is our hope that you have found inspiration, enlightenment, and valuable takeaways that resonate with you on your own quest for knowledge.

Remember that the pursuit of understanding is an ever-evolving journey, and this book is but a milestone along the way. The world of knowledge is vast and boundless, offering endless opportunities for exploration and growth.

As you conclude this book, we encourage you to carry forward the torch of curiosity and continue your exploration of these subjects. Seek out new perspectives, engage in meaningful discussions, and embrace the thrill of lifelong learning.

We express our sincere gratitude for joining us on this intellectual adventure. Your curiosity and dedication to expanding your horizons are the driving forces behind our shared quest for wisdom and insight.

Thank you for entrusting us with a portion of your intellectual journey. May your pursuit of knowledge lead you to new heights and inspire others to embark on their own quests for understanding.

With profound gratitude,

Nikhilesh Mishra, Author.

Appendices

Glossary of Data Science and Big Data Terms

1. Algorithm: A step-by-step procedure or set of rules for performing a specific task or solving a problem, often implemented in software to process and analyze data.

2. Analytics: The process of examining data to discover meaningful patterns, insights, and trends that inform decision-making and business strategies.

3. Anomaly Detection: Identifying data points or patterns that deviate significantly from the expected or normal behavior, often used for fraud detection or quality control.

4. Big Data: A term referring to large and complex datasets that exceed the processing capabilities of traditional data management tools, often characterized by the "4Vs": volume, variety, velocity, and veracity.

5. Business Intelligence (BI): Technologies, processes, and tools for collecting, analyzing, and presenting business-related data to support informed decision-making.

6. Clustering: A data analysis technique that groups similar data points together based on specific criteria, aiming to uncover inherent patterns or segments.

7. Data Cleaning: The process of identifying and correcting errors, inconsistencies, and inaccuracies in datasets to improve data quality.

8. Data Mining: Extracting useful and previously unknown information from large datasets by using statistical and computational techniques.

9. Data Science: An interdisciplinary field that uses scientific methods, algorithms, and systems to extract knowledge and insights from data.

10. Data Visualization: Presenting data and information in graphical or visual formats to aid understanding, exploration, and communication.

11. Exploratory Data Analysis (EDA): An approach to analyzing data to summarize its main characteristics, detect patterns, and identify anomalies or outliers.

12. Feature Engineering: The process of selecting, transforming, or creating relevant features (variables) from raw data to improve the performance of machine learning models.

13. Feature Selection: Identifying and selecting a subset of important features from the original dataset, aiming to improve model performance and reduce complexity.

14. Hypothesis Testing: A statistical method used to assess the

validity of assumptions or hypotheses about a population based on sample data.

15. Inferential Statistics: Techniques used to make predictions or draw conclusions about a population based on a sample of data.

16. Machine Learning: A subset of artificial intelligence that involves training algorithms to recognize patterns in data and make predictions or decisions without being explicitly programmed.

17. Natural Language Processing (NLP): The field of study that focuses on enabling computers to understand, interpret, and generate human language.

18. NoSQL: A category of database systems designed to handle unstructured, semi-structured, or rapidly changing data types, often used in big data applications.

19. Predictive Modeling: Creating and using mathematical and computational models to predict future outcomes or behaviors based on historical data.

20. Regression Analysis: A statistical method used to model the relationship between a dependent variable and one or more independent variables.

21. Supervised Learning: A type of machine learning where algorithms learn from labeled training data to make predictions or

classifications.

22. Unsupervised Learning: A type of machine learning where algorithms learn from unlabeled data to identify patterns or groupings.

23. Text Mining: The process of extracting valuable information, patterns, or insights from large volumes of textual data.

24. Validation: Assessing the performance and generalization of machine learning models using separate data from the training set.

25. Visual Analytics: Combining data visualization and interactive analytics to facilitate exploration and understanding of complex datasets.

This glossary provides an overview of key terms in the fields of data science and big data analytics. It's important to note that these fields are dynamic and continually evolving, so staying updated with emerging terms and concepts is essential for professionals in these domains.

Sample Data Analysis Projects

Embarking on data analysis projects is a pivotal step toward mastering the intricacies of data science and big data analytics. These projects not only consolidate your theoretical knowledge but also empower you to apply your skills to real-world scenarios. Below are a few illustrative sample data analysis projects that can serve as inspiration for your journey:

1. **Market Basket Analysis:** *Objective:* Explore customer purchasing patterns in a retail dataset to identify frequently co-occurring products. *Steps:* Data preprocessing, association rule mining, visualization of frequent itemsets, interpretation of results. *Skills Highlighted:* Data preprocessing, exploratory data analysis, association analysis.

2. **Predictive Customer Churn Analysis:** *Objective:* Build a predictive model to forecast customer churn for a subscription-based service. *Steps:* Data preprocessing, feature engineering, model selection (e.g., logistic regression, random forest), evaluation of model performance. *Skills Highlighted:* Feature engineering, predictive modeling, model evaluation.

3. **Sentiment Analysis of Social Media Data:** *Objective:* Analyze sentiments expressed in social media posts related to a specific topic or brand. *Steps:* Data collection from social media APIs, text preprocessing, sentiment analysis using

natural language processing techniques, visualization of sentiment trends. *Skills Highlighted:* Data collection, text preprocessing, sentiment analysis, data visualization.

4. **Time Series Forecasting for Financial Data:** *Objective:* Forecast stock prices or financial metrics using time series analysis. *Steps:* Data preprocessing, time series decomposition, model selection (e.g., ARIMA, LSTM), validation of forecasts. *Skills Highlighted:* Time series analysis, model selection, forecasting.

5. **Image Classification using Convolutional Neural Networks (CNNs):** *Objective:* Develop an image classifier to categorize objects within images. *Steps:* Data preprocessing, CNN architecture design, model training, evaluation of classification performance. *Skills Highlighted:* Deep learning, CNN architecture, image classification.

6. **Exploration of Health Data for Disease Patterns:** *Objective:* Analyze health-related datasets to uncover insights into disease prevalence, risk factors, and correlations. *Steps:* Data preprocessing, exploratory data analysis, correlation analysis, visualization of health trends. *Skills Highlighted:* Exploratory data analysis, data visualization, health domain knowledge.

7. **Recommendation System for E-Commerce:** *Objective:* Design a recommendation system to suggest products to users

based on their preferences and behavior. *Steps:* Data preprocessing, collaborative filtering or content-based filtering, evaluation of recommendation performance. *Skills Highlighted:* Recommendation systems, collaborative filtering, content-based filtering.

These sample projects provide a glimpse into the diverse applications of data analysis across various domains. As you embark on your own data analysis projects, remember to define clear objectives, follow best practices for data preprocessing, select appropriate analysis techniques, and interpret and communicate your findings effectively. The world of data analysis offers endless opportunities for exploration and innovation, allowing you to contribute meaningfully to solving complex challenges.

Feel free to adapt and customize these project ideas based on your interests, domain expertise, and the datasets at your disposal. By undertaking such projects, you'll not only refine your skills but also build a strong portfolio that showcases your expertise to potential employers, collaborators, and the broader data science community.

Data Science and Big Data Analytics Tools and Resources

Embarking on your journey to become a proficient data scientist requires a robust toolkit of tools and resources. Here, we delve into an extensive array of essential resources that can serve as your guide and companion in the realm of data science and big data analytics:

1. Programming Languages:

- **Versatile Languages:** Master widely-used languages like Python and R for data manipulation, analysis, and visualization.

2. Data Visualization:

- **Visualization Libraries:** Leverage Python libraries such as Matplotlib and Seaborn to create insightful data visualizations.

- **Interactive Dashboards:** Craft engaging visual narratives with tools like Plotly and Bokeh.

3. Machine Learning and Deep Learning Frameworks:

- **Framework Exploration:** Dive into frameworks like Scikit-Learn, TensorFlow, and PyTorch for building and training machine learning and deep learning models.

4. Big Data Technologies:

- **Data Processing:** Discover the power of distributed computing with Hadoop and Apache Spark for processing vast datasets.

- **NoSQL Databases:** Explore NoSQL databases for seamless management of unstructured data.

5. Data Cleaning and Preprocessing:

- **Data Transformation:** Utilize tools to clean, transform, and reshape data, ensuring it's ready for analysis.

6. Data Analytics and Visualization Platforms:

- **Interactive Notebooks:** Embrace Jupyter Notebooks for interactive data analysis and code documentation.

- **Visual Analytics:** Engage with platforms for creating captivating, interactive visualizations and dashboards.

7. Cloud Computing Platforms:

- **Cloud Infrastructure:** Tap into the power of cloud platforms to access scalable computing resources for data analysis.

8. Learning Platforms and Courses:

- **Educational Exploration:** Deepen your knowledge through online courses, books, and blogs, tailored to your learning pace and style.

- **Comprehensive Texts:** Immerse yourself in authoritative texts that unravel the intricacies of data science and big data analytics.

9. Data Repositories and Datasets:

- **Practice and Exploration:** Access diverse datasets for honing your skills and experimenting with real-world scenarios.

10. Professional Organizations and Communities:

- **Networking and Collaboration:** Join data science communities and professional organizations to connect with peers, share insights, and collaborate on projects.

11. Conferences and Meetups:

- **Industry Insights:** Participate in conferences and local meetups to stay updated on the latest trends and breakthroughs.

12. Research Journals and Publications:

- **Academic Insights:** Explore research journals that publish studies and findings related to data science and big data analytics.

13. Coding Repositories:

- **Open Source Contribution:** Engage with coding repositories to contribute to open-source projects and enhance your coding skills.

14. Forums and Discussion Boards:

- **Interactive Discussions:** Participate in online forums and discussion boards to seek advice, share experiences, and exchange ideas.

15. Professional Certifications:

- **Validation of Expertise:** Pursue certifications to validate your expertise and enhance your credibility in the data science field.

As you embark on your data science and big data analytics journey, remember that these tools and resources are your allies, aiding you in unraveling complex challenges, uncovering meaningful insights, and driving innovation. Embrace the spirit of continuous learning, experimentation, and exploration, and let **www.nikhileshmishra.com** serve as your portal to a world of limitless possibilities in the realm of data science and big data analytics.

Resources and References

As you reach the final pages of this book by Nikhilesh Mishra, consider it not an ending but a stepping stone. The pursuit of knowledge is an unending journey, and the world of information is boundless.

Discover a World Beyond These Pages

We extend a warm invitation to explore a realm of boundless learning and discovery through our dedicated online platform: **www.nikhileshmishra.com**. Here, you will unearth a carefully curated trove of resources and references to empower your quest for wisdom.

Unleash the Potential of Your Mind

- **Digital Libraries:** Immerse yourself in vast digital libraries, granting access to books, research papers, and academic treasures.

- **Interactive Courses:** Engage with interactive courses and lectures from world-renowned institutions, nurturing your thirst for knowledge.

- **Enlightening Talks:** Be captivated by enlightening talks delivered by visionaries and experts from diverse fields.

- **Community Connections:** Connect with a global community of like-minded seekers, engage in meaningful discussions, and share your knowledge journey.

Your Journey Has Just Begun

Your journey as a seeker of knowledge need not end here. Our website awaits your exploration, offering a gateway to an infinite universe of insights and references tailored to ignite your intellectual curiosity.

Acknowledgments

As I stand at this pivotal juncture, reflecting upon the completion of this monumental work, I am overwhelmed with profound gratitude for the exceptional individuals who have been instrumental in shaping this remarkable journey.

In Loving Memory

To my father, **Late Shri Krishna Gopal Mishra,** whose legacy of wisdom and strength continues to illuminate my path, even in his physical absence, I offer my deepest respect and heartfelt appreciation.

The Pillars of Support

My mother**, Mrs. Vijay Kanti Mishra,** embodies unwavering resilience and grace. Your steadfast support and unwavering faith in my pursuits have been the bedrock of my journey.

To my beloved wife, **Mrs. Anshika Mishra,** your unshakable belief in my abilities has been an eternal wellspring of motivation. Your constant encouragement has propelled me to reach new heights.

My daughter, **Miss Aarvi Mishra,** infuses my life with boundless joy and unbridled inspiration. Your insatiable curiosity serves as a constant reminder of the limitless power of exploration and discovery.

Brothers in Arms

To my younger brothers, **Mr. Ashutosh Mishra** and **Mr. Devashish Mishra,** who have steadfastly stood by my side, offering unwavering support and shared experiences that underscore the strength of familial bonds.

A Journey Shared

This book is a testament to the countless hours of dedication and effort that have gone into its creation. I am immensely grateful for the privilege of sharing my knowledge and insights with a global audience.

Readers, My Companions

To all the readers who embark on this intellectual journey alongside me, your curiosity and unquenchable thirst for knowledge inspire me to continually push the boundaries of understanding in the realm of cloud computing.

With profound appreciation and sincere gratitude,

Nikhilesh Mishra

August 18, 2023

About the Author

Nikhilesh Mishra is an extraordinary visionary, propelled by an insatiable curiosity and an unyielding passion for innovation. With a relentless commitment to exploring the boundaries of knowledge and technology, Nikhilesh has embarked on an exceptional journey to unravel the intricate complexities of our world.

Hailing from the vibrant and diverse landscape of India, Nikhilesh's pursuit of knowledge has driven him to plunge deep into the world of discovery and understanding from a remarkably young age. His unwavering determination and quest for innovation have not only cemented his position as a thought leader but have also earned him global recognition in the ever-evolving realm of technology and human understanding.

Over the years, Nikhilesh has not only mastered the art of translating complex concepts into accessible insights but has also crafted a unique talent for inspiring others to explore the limitless possibilities of human potential.

Nikhilesh's journey transcends the mere boundaries of expertise; it is a transformative odyssey that challenges conventional wisdom and redefines the essence of exploration. His commitment to pushing the boundaries and reimagining the norm serves as a luminous beacon of inspiration to all those who aspire to make a profound impact in the world of knowledge.

As you navigate the intricate corridors of human understanding and innovation, you will not only gain insight into Nikhilesh's expertise but also experience his unwavering dedication to empowering readers like you. Prepare to be enthralled as he seamlessly melds intricate insights with real-world applications, igniting the flames of curiosity and innovation within each reader.

Nikhilesh Mishra's work extends beyond the realm of authorship; it is a reflection of his steadfast commitment to shaping the future of knowledge and exploration. It is an embodiment of his boundless dedication to disseminating wisdom for the betterment of individuals worldwide.

Prepare to be inspired, enlightened, and empowered as you embark on this transformative journey alongside Nikhilesh Mishra. Your understanding of the world will be forever enriched, and your passion for exploration and innovation will reach new heights under his expert guidance.

Sincerely, **A Fellow Explorer**

Notes

Notes

Notes

Notes

Notes

Notes

Notes

Notes

Notes

Notes